YOUR MONEY
Straight and Simple

£ YOUR MONEY
Straight and Simple

ALISON MITCHELL

BBC BOOKS

*To my brother, George, with thanks
for all his help and encouragement
over the years.*

Published by BBC Books,
a division of BBC Enterprises Limited,
Woodlands, 80 Wood Lane, London W12 0TT
First published 1992
© Alison Mitchell 1992
The moral right of the author has been asserted
ISBN 0 563 36312 6

Set in 10½/11½pt Ehrhardt by
Phoenix Photosetting, Chatham, Kent

Printed and bound in Great Britain by
Clays Ltd, St Ives plc

Cover printed by Clays Ltd, St Ives plc

Contents

Acknowledgements

I am most grateful to all the specialists who helped with the laborious task of checking the facts in this book. So many of them took the time and trouble to read and check the chapters and return them promptly.

I am particularly indebted to Paddy Ross of the Leith Citizens Advice Bureau and her colleague, Joan Lord, who read and corrected many of the chapters on budgeting, debt and crisis times.

I also benefited from the help of Pauline Hedges at the British Bankers' Association; John Mayes at the Royal Bank of Scotland; Phil Reed at the Leeds Permanent Building Society; David Percival at National Savings; lawyers, Keith Deighton at the Glasgow firm of Bird Semple Fyfe Ireland, and Margaret Crabtree at the Barnes firm of Ashbys; tax accountant, Viscount Mackintosh of Halifax at Price Waterhouse; Margaret McLellan at Age Concern; Cecil Hinton of Hinton & Wild; Sue Anderson at the Building Societies' Association and Chris Bain at the Birmingham Settlement.

At *Bazaar*, producer Erica Griffiths and consultant Val Corbett have steered the money items with tact and imagination and have been a joy to work with.

Added to that has been the forbearance of my children, Laura and Jamie, and the help and encouragement of my husband Ronald.

Alison Mitchell

1 · *Your Money and You*

If our private dreams were made public, we would all want to be rich and famous. And if we could only have one wish, we would settle for just being rich. Winning the pools – then lying beside one deciding just how to spend one's fortune – must be most people's heart's desire.

This book will not instruct you on becoming a millionaire or provide a golden key to unlock the door to wealth beyond the dreams of avarice. But it will make your pocket a little deeper, your money go a little further and, consequently, your life seem a little happier.

It is often said that money can't buy you happiness. Maybe it can't. But all you want is to rent it for a lifetime. I have spent my working life writing about the rich and the poor. Take it from me – the rich are happier. Having financial security gives you peace of mind. And that is what I promise you in this book. From now on the colour of money will leave you happily in the pink, not floundering about in the red. Already, you are part of the way there. By picking up this book you have demonstrated that you want to put your financial affairs in order.

No one ever has enough money. It is the desire to pile it even higher that spurs tycoons on to yet another takeover, makes best-selling authors pen just one more blockbuster, or platinum-plated popstars cut a new album. And yet it has always been so. Even the ancient Romans had a Latin motto for this hunger for money: *satis superque* they called it – enough, and then a bit more.

Well, I am going to help you get it. By showing you how to manage your money, how to organise your financial affairs and how to control your cash, I am going to make you better off. And that is a promise.

You won't have any more coming in, indeed you might not even have any less going out, but financially you will feel more comfortable.

For the past 10 years I have been helping people like you to get on top of their finances. From my first phone in on BBC *Breakfast Time* to the current series of *Bazaar*, I have been offering advice and help. And it boils down to this: be in control of your cash – don't let it be in control of you.

Whether you live in a mansion or a maisonette, a castle or a cottage, you must know where you stand. How much do you owe? What are your savings standing at? Will cashing a cheque put you into overdraft? Can you afford the new stereo that you would like to buy? If you can't answer questions like that then you aren't in control. And if you aren't in control, you haven't a hope of ever knocking your finances into shape. So let's start by finding out how much you know about your own money.

Try this quiz to see if you are running your money or it is running you:

---

1 The washing machine has broken down and it costs £50 to fix. You write a cheque for the full amount. Does this put your current account in overdraft?
a) yes
b) no
c) haven't a clue

---

2 You bought a new outfit for a wedding you are going to and it cost more than you expected to pay. What will you do now?
a) ask at work to see if you can do more overtime this month
b) ring the bank to alert them to the expense and ask for a bigger overdraft
c) hope the bank manager won't notice if you don't tell him

---

3 The word TESSA has been in the financial press a lot lately, but do you know what it is?
a) a savings account for children
b) an account with tax advantages which offers increased savings rates
c) the name of the Chancellor's wife

---

4 A friend's 14-year-old son wants to open a savings account. He is plumping for a bank account because he gets a free camera when he puts in his first £10. He thinks he won't pay tax on the interest and asks your advice. Would you tell him
a) choose National Savings instead to get the interest gross
b) it doesn't matter where he puts the money because he is not a tax payer anyway
c) he is right so long as he fills in a tax exemption form when he opens the account

---

5 Good news for home owners – the mortgage rate has just come down one per cent from 14 per cent to 13 per cent. You have a mortgage of £30000. This gives you a monthly saving of
a) £10
b) £40
c) £100

---

6 Your daughter has just bought a new stereo on credit. The bank wanted to lend her the money at a fixed annual rate of 11 per cent but if she put it on her credit card it would cost two per cent per month. Which is cheaper over a year?
a) the bank
b) the credit card
c) don't know

7 Do you know what the balance or overdraft is on your current account to the nearest £20?
a) yes
b) no

8 Your credit card limit has been reached and you are offered an increased limit by the card company. Do you
a) accept the offer – it means you will have more money to spend
b) turn them down – you know you won't be able to make the minimum payments on the new limit
c) disregard the offer – you have just been accepted for another card with an even bigger limit.

Your score:
1 a2; b1; c3
2 a1; b2; c3
3 a3; b1; c3
4 a2; b3; c1
5 a2; b1; c3
6 a1; b2; c3
7 a1; b3
8 a3; b1; c3

How did you fare?
8–12 You certainly know where you stand with your money – and that is a good first step to knocking it into shape.

13–19 You have a little knowledge of what is going on and need to know more. Take care not to let things slip further.

20–24 You are in the danger zone. If you are not careful you could tail spin out of control so get a grip of things now.

Thousands of people slip from credit into debt every year. They think they are able to make the payments and keep on top but things get out of hand. Often through no fault of their own they find they have built up huge unrepayable debts without realising it. Thousands more fail to take full advantage of all the financial perks going because they just don't know about them, or think they apply to someone else.

Well, I am going to make sure that everything that is going is coming to you, and that you don't make the financial mistakes others might.

Start at the beginning of this book, and go at whatever speed you choose. Find your own level. Some of you might choose to read *Your Money Straight and Simple* from start to finish. Others will dip in at the parts they will find most useful. But I guarantee that, no matter what your level, you will be better off at the end.

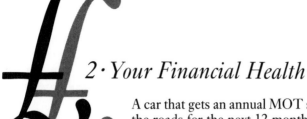

2 · Your Financial Health

A car that gets an annual MOT should be safe on the roads for the next 12 months. The mechanic tests all the working parts, looks over the body work, fixes what is broken or not running properly and passes it. Much the same can be said about a medical check-up. A doctor gives you all the tests he thinks you need to ensure that your organs are functioning as they should.

Well, I am going to do the same for your money. I will help you to run a test over the various aspects of your finances – do it every year and it should keep everything ticking over nicely. Anything that shows up as a problem can be fixed – by reading the necessary chapter later in the book. And, as with cars and bodies, the sooner you discover and solve the problem, the less damage will be done.

FINANCIAL HEALTH CHECK

Your finances can be broken down into two separate parts:

- incomings
- outgoings

Incomings

This is just a posh word for the money you have coming into the household every week. It could be from your salary, or your partner's, a pension, interest on any savings you have, child benefit or any other DSS benefits.

Salary Every week or month, when you get your wages, you will also get a pay slip. Check it. They can be wrong. Payslips don't conform to any simple layout. They are all different. The only thing they have in common is that they contain much the same information and they are difficult to read. But persevere. Not every month if you feel that is too much, but at least once a year. What your payslip shows is how much you earn, including overtime and bonuses less deductions for tax, national insurance, pension, perhaps repaying a company loan. That brings you down to net pay, and net pay is what you take home every week or month. Run your eye over the other details too, such as your employee number and tax code. If they are wrong, you could be getting less than you should. The Inland Revenue deals with the tax code (further details page 84), and your employer will cope with any other queries.

The boxes you don't understand – perhaps labelled 'Adj' or 'Others' –

will have a code that is explained at the bottom of the payslip, or over the page. But if that doesn't clear it up so that you fully understand what is being added on and taken off, then you should ring the wages department and get them to explain it to you.

Pensions Most companies pay their pensioners monthly, probably into a bank or building society account. Check that annual increases – if there are any – come on the due date. It is also worth finding out what your wife will get should you, the pensioner, die. (Husbands seldom get anything from a wife's pension!) Many company schemes pay the widow half the pension, but that can be more than it seems because it may be half the original pension before any lump sum was taken out. Write and ask, because once you know you may need to take some financial action if it is going to be less, or more, than you thought.

Interest on savings Whether you have £100, £1000 or £10000 put aside for a rainy day, make sure it is earning a top rate of interest. You work hard for your money, so make sure it is working hard for you.

First, ask yourself what you want from your savings. Easy access, good rates of interest. Are you always using the account by taking money out and putting it back or does it lie dormant ready for holidays, Christmas or emergencies? Once you know that, you will know if it is in the right sort of account. Read Chapters 7 and 8 to find out what is on offer and move your money if you are in the wrong place.

Getting an extra one per cent on savings of £1000 doesn't seem much. But the extra £10 would buy you a celebratory bottle of champagne, or pay for all the Christmas wrapping paper you need.

Child Benefit If you have children, you get Child Benefit. At the moment it is £8.25 a week for the first child, and £7.25 for every other child you have. But what happens to that money? Does it just disappear into the common family budget or do you reserve it to try and use the money for the children? There are no rights or wrongs on this, so long as you know what is happening to the money. After all, if you have two children you are receiving over £800 a year from the DSS, so don't let it just slip through your fingers.

Outgoings
This is the money that you spend every week – to run the house, pay for everything you need, even go into the savings accounts you have.

For most of us, this is the area that is too fat. No matter how much you earn, your spending will keep up. Lifestyles always seem to follow the wage. You never quite have enough to get by on. So let's trim your debts, and learn to keep your spending habits in trim.

If you have ever been on a diet then you will know most of what there is to know about controlling your finances. You don't think so?

Take the basic rules of slimming.

- *Keep to 1000 calories a day* It is the same with money – you have to know your spending limits. Most people let too much slip through their fingers on simply living from day to day. Just as fatties nibble throughout the day without realising what they have eaten, so you buy little bits and pieces that all add up. Your paper in the morning, a magazine to read on the train or bus, the odd can of coke or a sandwich for the office, a little toy or packet of sweets for the children, a paperback, new lipstick, a pint or two in the pub. If you think I am wrong, just keep your own tally of extras for a day or two. I am not saying you should cut them all out, just control them. Choose a spending level that is right for your budget and restrict yourself to that every day. If you go over, cut back the next day and you will be surprised how much this saves you.

- *Avoid impulse eating* And impulse spending. You see a pair of shoes, a book, some CDs, perhaps even a new stereo and you buy it. Regardless of what it is, it sears right through your attempts to budget and it can take months to pay off the debt.

  Control yourself – and don't buy it. Any large purchases should be financially planned for and the small ones should be within your daily spending limit.

> *TIP* · If you are an avid impulse buyer don't take too much money or plastic with you on your shopping trips. That way you have to make a return trip to get what you wanted – and you have time to exercise your will power.

- *Save up for a celebration* Dieters going out for a slap-up meal have to save up the calories in advance. Do the same with money. There is nothing wrong with saving before spending, old-fashioned as that might sound. And it gives you two additional bonuses. You get interest on the money you have saved so that by the time you come to spend it there is a little more in the account than you expected. And you won't have massive interest payments to cope with.

- *Regular weigh-ins control your weight* And regular checking of statements keeps you in control of your budget. If you don't know how much you have in your account, you won't know if you are overspending and running into overdraft. Keep a tight grip on the figures and the monthly credit card bills won't come as a shock.

- *Don't give up if you have a disaster* If you overeat today, go back on the diet tomorrow. All you need are a few lean days to get back to where you were. A bit of overspending needs the same cure. Cut out all the extras over the next few days and you will claw back anything that you let slip through your fingers.

- *Keep a notice pinned to the fridge door* 'A moment on the lips, a lifetime on the hips,' to stop you nibbling. You could do a lot worse than having something similar stuck onto your credit card: 'Buy in a second, bigger debts than you reckon'd.'

I once saw a notice pinned to the door of a slimming club – 'If dissatisfied, your fat can always be refunded.' The same can be said about your muddled money. If you don't feel more in charge of your cash after you have spent a day of reckoning, you can always let it muddle itself up again. But, I bet you don't.

3 · Controlling Your Cash

Controlling your cash is not a talent you are born with. It is not even a skill you learn at school. It is a very simple exercise that anyone can do – that everyone should do – and it will make a huge difference to your life.

All you really need to get you started are a sharp pencil and a clean sheet of paper. For what you are about to do is work out where you and your money stand. It is a bit like taking a snapshot of your financial affairs. It won't really tell you what has been happening or what will happen in the future, but it will give you a very clear idea of exactly where you are now. And it will point you towards any action that you should take to sort out minor problems before they become major.

BUDGET

Think of the word 'Budget' and it conjures up a picture of the Chancellor of the Exchequer holding aloft his old red dispatch case on his way to the Commons. That is not a bad image. For what you need to do to your finances is a small-scale version of what he does for the country – balance the books.

But before you do that you will have to know what you have coming in – and that is the easy part – and what is going out. So, let's start with the simple part. Turn to the Budget Planner overleaf and fill in the columns marked Incomings.

Coming In

That is your wages, pensions, interest on savings and any DSS benefits, such as Child Benefit that you have. If you have any other source of income – a wealthy uncle, perhaps, who sends you monthly cheques – add it on.

Going Out

When it comes to what you spend your money on, that is a bit trickier. Some of the columns are relatively easy. You should know, or at least be able to find out, about the bigger payments you make such as the mortgage or rent, insurance, community charge, season ticket, gas and electricity, car insurance and so on. But the rest is more difficult. There is no point in just guessing what you spend in a week. So here is what to do. Write it down. It sounds tedious but in fact it can be quite fun.

Budget Planner

INCOMINGS	what you get	per month
Your salary		
Partner's salary		
Any other salary		
Interest on savings		
Pension		
Partner's pension		
Child Benefit		
DSS benefit		
Other money		

OUTGOINGS (Regular)	what you pay	per month
Mortgage		
Rent		
Community charge		
House Insurance		
Gas		
Electricity		
Coal/Oil/Calor gas		
Water Rates		
Season ticket/fares		
Car Tax		
TV licence		
Phone		
Car Insurance/MOT		

OUTGOINGS (Everyday)	what you pay	per month
Supermarket		
Local shops		
School meals		
Clothes and shoes		
Newspapers and milk		
Petrol/local fares		
Magazines		
Extras		

OUTGOINGS (Occasional)	what you pay	per month
Presents		
House		
Garden		
Children's treats		
Hobby		
Holiday		
Christmas		
Sport		
Replacement purchases		
Repair bills		
Extras		
OUTGOINGS (Savings)		
Life insurance		
Savings plan		
Interest on loans		
HP payments		
Credit Union		
TOTAL		
Incomings monthly total		
Outgoings monthly total		
Difference		

Spending Diary Every time you spend anything mark it down in a note book. No matter how little it seems at the time, add it on so that you have a complete record in your spending diary at the end of the week, of what you have spent. It is better to do it for a fortnight, but few of us have the discipline to do that. At the end of the period, don't just add up the total, look to see where the money has gone. It will highlight clearly if you are overspending on any one area. Maybe you have lunch out every day which costs a lot more than you expected, or you take more taxis than you should, or your magazine bill is higher than it ought to be, or you are keeping the local publican in holidays to Torremolinos.

I am not suggesting that you should cut all these things out, but just be aware of where your cash is going so that if you hit a lean patch you will know exactly where savings can be made.

It will also show up your spending pattern. You may spend a lot in your lunch hour because you wander round the shops, or most of your spending is done at the weekends. Or you buy expensive snacks in the canteen, instead of bringing an apple or a bag of crisps from home.

Once you see what it is that triggers the spending, you are over half way to stopping yourself doing it.

> *TIP* · There is another advantage to keeping a spending diary for a week – you will spend less. Just because you are writing it all down you will avoid some purchases, so there will be a bonus in your purse or wallet at the end of the week.

Once you have worked out what you spend casually in a week, have a go at filling in the rest of the Budget Planner. You might have to check back on a few gas and electricity bills to come up with an average monthly figure and remember that your summer bills will be a lot lower than your winter bills because the weather is warmer, so don't cheat and write in an August figure. To save you looking it up – a colour TV licence is currently £77 while car tax is £100 a year.

I have included a 'replacement' space because every year there is at least one major item in the house that needs renewing. Whether it is the washing machine, a carpet, new curtains, the lawnmower, budget for it and you won't feel so badly about it when you have to do the spending.

> *TIP* · To make this job easier for the future, try to keep all your receipts and bills in one file or box. If you have to spend three hours rooting around looking for the papers you will go off the idea of budgeting before you ever get started.

Now, when you get to the end, cross your fingers that the Incomings are higher than the Outgoings. If they are, then you are in clover and can start to really try and save some money every month.

But if they are not – and I suspect for most of us that the Outgoings are the larger figure – then you will have to do something about it.

It is a simple choice really:
■ increase the incomings
■ decrease the outgoings

■ *Increase the incomings* Since we can't just print our own fivers, you will have to do something positive here. Perhaps take in a lodger, work more overtime, maybe your partner can take a part time job, or increase the hours worked to full time. Check to see if you can claim any benefits, such as Family Credit, from the DSS. Maybe you have a wage rise in the pipeline at work which will help in the months to come. But if none of these fit your circumstances then you will have to move on to the other option.

> *TIP* · If a husband works and a wife doesn't then it's crucial that any savings you do have are in her name. She gets a tax free allowance the same as anyone else so she can set the tax on the interest against it. That way, she will get the equivalent of a quarter more interest on the money. For further details see Chapter 10.

■ *Decrease the outgoings* Take a look at your figures section by section. Most regular outgoings are almost impossible to reduce. After all it would be difficult to stop paying the rent, or decide against funding the TV licence. That would end up costing you more than you saved. And cancelling the house insurance policy would be a false economy.

If really drastic measures are called for, however, you might have to think about getting rid of the car. According to the AA it costs around £4000 a year to run an average family saloon car – taking into account depreciation, car tax, insurance, petrol and so on. So you would make a substantial saving by ditching your wheels. Not only would you be able to sell the car and get a large lump sum for that, but you would save on the insurance, car tax, petrol and repair bills.

However, don't just take that whole amount off the total. You will have to add in a figure for fares and possibly taxis. Few people, who are used to driving to the supermarket, would relish carrying £50 of groceries home on the bus so a weekly taxi fare from the supermarket might have to be budgeted for. But selling the car is a bit drastic. Try keeping a record of how long you spend on the phone to friends and family for a week. You will find you could cut that down. Or check your gas and electricity consumption. Heating the water for a shower costs a lot less than for a bath.

Your 'everyday' expenses might reduce a bit – particularly the extras which come from the weekly tally you have just kept. Have a good inspection of that list and see where the savings can be made – then make them.

The 'occasional' list is probably the real shocker. When you sit down and think about it you probably spend a good deal on presents, treats, holidays, the house and the garden. Worse than that, you have most likely forgotten to add in the money you spend on cards, wrapping paper, stamps and so on. Start taking on board some of the hints and tips you get on DIY – from wrapping paper (felt tip a pattern on lining paper) to making your own curtains.

For many people it is enough just to have filled in this Budget Planner. Once they see where the leaks are they can do something to staunch them. But if your financial problems are more serious than that, turn to Chapter 6 to find out what your next step will be.

Budging the bills   Once you have balanced your books the next step is easy. But if you don't take it you could find your budget is knocked sideways by an unexpected bill.

This is something that happens to all of us – usually in January. You have a good Christmas, but you spend more than you should. Probably on credit cards, charge cards and by writing cheques. Come January, and the moment of truth arrives. The bills fall due and you can't pay. Well you could, if you had nothing else to pay that month. Or you find that one month in the year is a particularly heavy one because, not only do you have the quarterly gas, electricity and phone bills to pay, but your annual season ticket needs renewing, the house insurance falls due and the TV licence has to be paid. Even something as simple as gas and electricity bills fox us every year. We all know that the March bill is always higher than the September one for the simple fact that winters in this country are colder than summers. But do we budget for these higher bills – we do not.

The answer is to try and stop bills from 'bunching'. Move the ones that you can to easier months and try to leave January as free as possible in order to cope with Christmas and the sales.

Cash calendar   Start by filling in the Cash Calendar opposite. Under 'Bills', write the bills you expect to pay in that month – gas, electricity, phone, insurance, car insurance, TV licence, car tax, season tickets, community charge, club membership and so on. In the other column 'Cash' write in any cheques you expect that are not regular income, for example, interest on savings accounts.

A quick glance at the calendar will show you which are the bad months. These are the ones to split up. Some things you cannot move. When your car tax comes due, you have to pay the full 6- or 12-month bill, so that one has to stay. But others can be bumped on. Take an annual season ticket, for example. If it falls in a bad period, it might be worthwhile buying a one month season, or even a three-month season, to move it into an area of the

Cash Calendar

Month	Bills	Cash
JANUARY		
FEBRUARY		
MARCH		
APRIL		
MAY		
JUNE		
JULY		
AUGUST		
SEPTEMBER		
OCTOBER		
NOVEMBER		
DECEMBER		

year where it is more affordable. Or try asking for a loan from work which will pay for the season in full and which you pay off over 12 months. Plenty of firms do them nowadays.

Try to pay bills monthly, if you can, rather than annually if it isn't going to cost you any more. The payment of community charge bills, for example, can be made on a monthly basis, as can some insurance premiums. But check first that there is no additional charge for this service.

TIP · Pay the milk and papers regularly – before they mount up to huge amounts. A fiver a week doesn't feel nearly as bad as £20 a month, does it?

Once you have got the calendar sorted out, draw one up for yourself, putting in the bills you expect against the appropriate month. Look at it regularly so that you know in advance what is coming up. That way you will be able to budget for the big bills and not be caught short.

Put on it the date that your building society and bank interest falls due, and tick it off when it comes in. That way you run a check against them forgetting about you or sending the money to someone else.

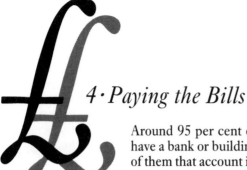

4 · Paying the Bills

Around 95 per cent of the adults in this country have a bank or building society account. For most of them that account is the basic budgeting tool of their financial life. When they are in funds they pay the extra into the account – or leave it there – and when times are tight they take the money out again. When things get desperate – they overdraw.

If you work, the chances are that you are one of the 40 million people with a current account – that is the one that comes with at least a chequebook and a guarantee card. And you will use that account to pay most of your bills. It is a good way of running your finances if you conform to the standard of being paid a salary into the bank account and using the facilities the account offers to pay your other bills. So let's just see what you get for your money.

How a Bank or Building Society Current Account Works

Most current accounts are used a lot. Every month there will be anything from a dozen to 20 or 30 different transactions, paying money in, and taking it out to pay other bills. For most people the main funding comes from their wage, or even two if a couple run a joint account.

At least once a month, you will have a very healthy balance on your account when your salary goes in. The day or two before it is due, you probably have very little left. Your mortgage or rent will take a hefty slice out. You might have standing orders, direct debits, debit card transactions, you will write cheques, take money out of the account through a 'hole in the wall' machine (more properly termed an ATM) and perhaps even dip into the red.

Cheques A cheque is merely a formal version of an IOU. You write the cheque and the recipient takes it along to the bank and gets the money for it. Providing you have cash in your account, or an overdraft facility, then the cheque will be cashed. You can write the cheque for any amount, but it is only guaranteed up to the level on your cheque guarantee card. This used to be a universal £50, but that figure is now rising on some accounts to £100 or even £250. However, in places like supermarkets where a £50 limit is constantly being broken, an honest face, writing your name and address on the back and some extra ID usually gets the cheque accepted.

Bouncing cheques If you don't have the funds in your account, or you are over your overdraft limit, the bank might refuse to cover your cheque. This is called 'bouncing'. It is not only embarrassing, but it is expensive as the bank will write to tell you it has bounced your cheque, and may charge £5 to £10 for the letter on top of the £15 or so it will charge for bouncing the cheque. A cheque covered by a guarantee card is never bounced.

> *TIP* · Never, ever, allow yourself to go into the red without setting up an overdraft facility first. Your bank will charge you a lot more in interest – up to 10 per cent in some cases.

Debit card This looks like a credit card, but acts like a cheque. Often with a fancy name like Switch or Connect a debit card replaces a cheque if the shop, garage or restaurant has the appropriate machine. The card is swiped through the machine, you sign the chit, and a day or two later your current account is debited for the amount. No more bulky chequebooks or being hampered by a £50 limit. And they are catching on fast.

Standing Order If you have a regular payment to make monthly or quarterly or even annually, and the amount doesn't vary, you can do it through a standing order. It is often used for paying mortgages, rent, community charge or subscriptions. You tell the bank how much the standing order is for, and to whom it is going and they make the payment on the appropriate day. If the amount changes – for example when the mortgage rate has gone down – notify the bank and they will change the standing order. But give them plenty of notice, particularly if the payment is made on the first day of the month.

Direct Debit This is similar to a standing order, but it is used for paying bills where the amount varies. Gas, phone and electricity bills and credit cards and insurance premiums are often paid this way. The company you owe money to is allowed, through the direct debit, to take the money out of your account. It is not ideal if you are budgeting on tight margins. Although you have to be told, in advance, how much is being taken out it is more difficult to budget with direct debits than cheques. So if you don't like direct debits, insist on being sent a bill in the usual way, and write a cheque to pay it.

WATCH OUT – If you close an account, remember to cancel all direct debits. They don't stop automatically just because you have closed the account, so you could find an unexpected bill following you around.

ATMs Automatic Teller Machines are the ones you use either inside or outside the bank or building society, using a plastic card and PIN number. Originally installed to allow customers to get cash quickly and easily they are now much more sophisticated. You can do a host of other things like checking your balance, getting a statement, transferring cash between two accounts, sometimes even leaving messages for the manager. There is often a letterbox for paying in too. Don't give your PIN number to anyone or you will be liable for any money they take out. And don't do as I did – write down your number in case you forget it. The thief who took my card – and the conveniently written-down number – also took £200 out of my account.

If you can change your number to a more easily-remembered one, then do.

TIP · If you use an ATM, keep the receipt to check against your bank statement otherwise you might forget and dip into overdraft by mistake.

Statement Every month you should get a bank statement. Some banks only send statements every three or even six months unless you ask for them more frequently. Ask. Monthly statements are crucial in keeping you on the straight and narrow.

The statement shows what has happened to your account in the past month: what has gone in, what has gone out and how much is left. It will also detail any charges. And check your statement, otherwise there is no point in having it. Mark off the cheques, standing orders and direct debits, and check that all the ATM transactions were yours. Watch out if you are in danger of slipping into the red. Try to keep your spending in hand until your salary is paid in so that you don't incur charges.

Charges Providing you keep in credit, your bank probably won't make any charges on your current account. Not only that, it will add interest to the money you have in the account. Not a lot, but every little helps. Some people still have the old-style non-interest paying current accounts. If you are one move your money now.

The variations, however, on that basic theme are enormous. So choose the one that suits you best. In general the accounts that are most generous on overdrafts offer less interest. If the interest rate is high, you won't do so well on the overdraft. So which are you? The type that slips into the red most months, or the type which keeps too large a sum in your current account.

At the top end you can have a current account, offering all the services, and linked to a high interest account. When your current account breaches an agreed level, say £500, then the extra is automatically transferred to the high interest account. If you write a large cheque, then cash will automatically be transferred back. That is called getting the best of both worlds. Other cheque accounts have tiered or banded interest rates, so that the more you keep in your accounts, the higher the rate you get.

At the other end, if you find that you are always slightly overspent at the end of every month, then choose an account that charges a flat monthly charge on an overdraft of over say £1000. You will, of course, have to pay interest on the money borrowed too. If you do breach the overdraft level, you will start to pay bank charges. And they can be a lot higher than you expected.

Bank charges are the dark side of getting interest on a current account. Slip into the red and you pay for all the services you have used in the period – usually one month or three months. They can be hefty. You can pay 20p to 40p per transaction and have a maintenance charge of £3 and upwards a quarter deducted from your account.

So make a huge effort not to dip into the red. And if you do, write fewer cheques that month.

TIP · Customers who seldom dip into the red and feel they have been grossly overcharged, should write to their bank manager pointing this out. Most bank charges are set by head office, but some are at the discretion of the manager. You might, if you are lucky, get them reduced.

Avoid bank charges by:
- staying in credit
- knowing when standing orders and direct debits fall due
- not writing cheques which will push you into the red

Budget Accounts

These bank accounts are specifically designed to help people to budget their household accounts. But they can be costly. They work like this:
You, and the bank, add together your annual household bills. Divide the total by 12 and assume that is the cost of running your house every month. This amount will be transferred every month from your current account. When the bills come in, you pay them using the chequebook that comes with this account. Because of the bunching of bills you often need more than the monthly sum – this is where you might come unstuck if you had an

ordinary current account. With a Budget account you are allowed to overdraw up to two or three times your limit.

For example:
Assume a total running cost of £4000 a year
That gives a monthly cost of £333.
In a particularly heavy month you might be able to pay bills of up to £999 – providing the bills you are paying were on the original list.

To pay for this account there is normally a flat fee, charged annually. You will also have to pay interest when the account is in debit, but you will get interest if the amount is in credit. Unless you really feel you need the comfort of this type of budgeting you should steer clear of it and budget for yourself.

Phone and fuel bills

Phone, gas and electricity bills are always larger than you expect. Coming quarterly, they are substantial sums for a household to pay. Don't despair – they all have budget schemes to help you, so use the one that suits you best.

Gas Paying your gas bill monthly smooths out the big bills. British Gas simply total the last four quarterly bills you have had, divide the answer by 12 and charge you that amount every month. You will be encouraged to pay by direct debit, but if you prefer, opt to pay by cheque or cash. At the end of the year, they will add up what the gas you have used actually costs and either make an extra charge, or refund the excess. In the meantime, you can buy stamps – £1 and £5 – from local gas shops to put towards your bill (if you pay by cash).

> *TIP* · Start a monthly payment scheme in the autumn. That way your bills are subsidised by British Gas because winter bills are higher than summer ones. If you start the scheme in the spring you subsidise them over the summer months.

Telephone British Telecom also run a monthly payments scheme. But it differs in one respect. They don't have an annual day of reckoning when they balance the books and charge or refund you. They do it every three months.

After looking at previous bills, BT will come up with a monthly charge. But every quarter you will get a statement showing what calls you have made and what the actual charge was. Along with the statement, will come

Cutting the cost of your phone

- Don't dial Directory Enquiries if you can avoid it – it costs 45p a time.

- Don't hang on if someone's extension is engaged – ring back. Listening to the music costs you money.

- Telephone after 6.00 pm, or before 8.00 am, it is cheaper.

- Make daytime calls after 1.00 pm, or between 8.00 am and 9.00 am, when it is the standard rate charge that applies.

- If you dial correctly but are connected incorrectly, ring the operator and ask for a credit.

- Don't ask the operator to connect you unless you are in difficulty. These calls are much more expensive.

- If you are ringing in peak time to a large organisation, try asking them to ring you back with the information, rather than holding on.

- Don't ring Australia on a Bank Holiday Monday and expect to get the call on cheap rate. That has been discontinued. Only weekends, Christmas and Boxing Day and New Year's Day are off-peak.

- After 6.00 pm here is not necessarily off-peak there, so check with the operator that the cheap rate applies to your call before you dial internationally.

- Get an itemised statement with your bill, if possible. And check it.

- Don't allow your children (or yourself) to make expensive calls to chat lines. Modern exchanges allow you to block these 0898 calls. Check with your operator.

- Don't rent a phone from BT. Buy your own – often for less than a tenner – instead of paying £4.47 a quarter in rent. BT will send you a jiffy bag so that you can return their phone free of charge.

TIP · BT are trying to find ways to allow new subscribers to spread the cost of getting a phone installed. It currently amounts to almost £150, so ask to see if a system has been set up.

a re-adjusted monthly figure, taking into account what you owe them (or they owe you) and averaging up or down the previous year's calls.

Customers with a modern exchange can also ask for an itemised statement. Get one if you can. This details every call that costs more than 44p: it tells you who you phoned, when and how much the call cost. You can then check that you (or someone using your phone) made that call. This will stop teenage children or their friends ever using your phone while you are out – and it will cut down your calls too. Seeing how much you spend chatting to friends and relatives, does wonders for the length of the next call.

You can also buy BT stamps to help pay the bill when it comes in. Available from the Post Office for £1.

Electricity Unlike the gas or phone, your electricity bill does not come from one nationwide company. Electricity is sold to you by your local company, so the budgeting schemes, although in general the same, may differ in the finer detail.

All the electricity companies offer a monthly payment scheme, by direct debit or standing order through a bank or building society account. As with the gas scheme, your previous year's bills will be totalled, and divided by 12 and you pay that as a monthly payment. You will continue to get quarterly statements so you will know if you are paying over or under and at the end of the year an adjustment will be made to the next year's payments to take in any deficit or over-payment.

If you prefer, you could make the payments in person in your local shop; and it doesn't have to be monthly. You could opt for weekly or fortnightly payments if that would help you to keep up. There is even a pay-as-you-go arrangement on offer, which means you can pay in as much as you like, when you like and this will be taken off your bill.

Energy Stamps are sold at electricity shops and local offices and these can be redeemed against your bill. And there are prepayment meters for those who don't want a bill at all. The old coin-in-the-slot meters are all but phased out by now and in their place have come electronic devices using a chargeable key or plastic card.

TIP · If you heat your home through storage heaters or need a lot of hot water in the mornings, find out about Economy 7. It is ideal for people who can use electricity overnight when it is offered at a cheaper rate. But you do have a larger quarterly standing charge so make sure your savings are large enough to cover that.

Can't Pay

If the bills are so large that you really can't pay, tell them. The fuel and telephone companies are used to dealing with this sort of problem, particularly after a hard winter, and have systems worked out to help.

Big bills can be spread to help you to pay them, but this can only be done if the company knows you have a problem. Ring the phone number on your bill and ask for advice on payment arrangements for people having difficulty paying. The longer you leave telling them, the more difficult it is for the company to help you. But if you feel you can't face handling this by yourself, get the help of a money counsellor. Your local Citizens' Advice Bureau is a good place to start. And read Chapter 6 for further advice.

5 · How to Borrow Money

A generation ago, borrowing money was regarded as somehow sinful. 'Neither a borrower nor a lender be' we were told. If, like me, you were brought up in Scotland it was a double sin. People who had to borrow money were only one step away from the poor house! Indeed, until quite recently, credit card companies and banks had to run different advertising campaigns in Scotland to persuade people that having a credit card really wouldn't lead them along the path of wickedness.

But times change. To borrow money is no longer a cardinal sin, indeed most of us wouldn't manage without a loan or two. Borrowing money can be a distinct advantage when controlling your finances. Few people could buy a home of their own without a mortgage, and that is no more than a long term loan.

Taking advantage of a good buy can save you pounds. You may see a real bargain in the summer or January sales that would suit you ideally, but you can't afford it. Take out a loan, or put it on a credit card and you might save a lot more than you pay in interest.

Borrowing money is a basic budgeting tool. You may not ever be able to afford £400 for a new washing machine. But you can afford, say, £40 a month. Save first and you will have to wait almost a year for it. Put it on HP or with a personal loan, still paying £40 a month, and you have it now, though you will be paying for longer than 10 months.

Old-fashioned Values

It is worth remembering here, though, that there is nothing wrong with saving up for something and then buying it outright. Good old-fashioned values stopped a lot of people from wrecking their lives by getting into debt. People who save first and pay cash, pay a lot less, because there are no interest payments.

TIP · If you can't afford something and need credit, find out the monthly repayments. Save that amount for two months and then make your purchase. This has two advantages. It proves that you can afford to make the payments, and it gives you a large deposit which means you borrow less and pay less interest. And you only have to wait two months, which is not too bad.

But how good are you at borrowing – do you get the best deal around? Try this quiz to see how you fare:

---

1 The cheapest form of borrowing is a bank overdraft?
a) yes
b) no
c) don't know

---

2 The longer you borrow for, the higher is the rate of interest?
a) yes
b) no
c) don't know

---

3 To compare interest rates, you should look at the APR?
a) yes
b) no
c) don't know

---

4 Borrowing from a loan shark is all right in an emergency?
a) yes
b) no
c) don't know

---

5 If you can't pay all your bills one month, should you pay your credit card bill before your mortgage?
a) yes
b) no
c) don't know

---

6 Getting a loan from the bank is cheaper than buying on HP?
a) yes
b) no
c) don't know

---

7 If you guarantee a loan for someone, and they default, do you have to make the payments?
a) yes
b) no
c) don't know

---

8 If you die owing money, and leave nothing else, your widow/er or children will have to pay off the debt?
a) yes
b) no
c) don't know

Correct Answers
1 b
2 b
3 a
4 b
5 b
6 a
7 a
8 b

Award yourself two points for every correct answer, and take off a point if you got questions 4 or 5 wrong.

12–16 You are doing well on the borrowing front. Provided you don't take on too large a commitment you should be OK.

8–12 Have a care, you are not getting the best deal every time you borrow money. Take a close look at the questions you got wrong and use this chapter to put you onto the right lines.

Less than 8 You are leaping before you look and going for the first loan you come to. That means you are paying too much in interest. Read on, it will save you money.

APR These three letters make or break your borrowing deal. They stand for the words Annual Percentage Rate, and how they are calculated matters not a jot.

What is important is that the APR is the rate you use to compare interest rates. By law, anyone offering interest, either on a loan or a deposit, has to quote the rate as an APR. So if you are not sure whether to buy your new cooker with a personal loan offering a flat rate of 10 per cent, an overdraft of 17.5 per cent, putting it on a credit card where the interest is two per cent a month, or taking out HP offering repayments of £56 a month check out the APR. You will see at a glance which is cheapest.

WHERE TO BORROW MONEY

There is no 'best way' to borrow money. Where you go for the loan depends on how long you want the money for, how much the loan is and how much of a hurry you are in when you buy. So, let me outline the options so that you can choose what is best for you.

Overdraft

What it is An overdraft is a flexible bank loan that runs on your current account. If you write a cheque knowing you don't have enough money to cover it, your account will move into the red and you will have what is known as an overdraft. It can vary from a few pounds to hundreds or even thousands. Make sure you set the arrangement up first, before you need it, or you may not get an overdraft. The bank might bounce your cheques instead.

When to use it An overdraft is ideal if you are only going to need the loan for a few days or weeks, perhaps until your salary goes into the bank again. It is too expensive to use if you are intending borrowing the money for a month or two. With some accounts, an overdraft will automatically push you into bank charges and that will add considerably to your monthly costs.

What it costs An arranged overdraft costs around four to five per cent above base rate depending on what sort of customer you are. The more business you give your bank the more you can shave off your interest rate. The interest is calculated daily so you pay less for short loans than you would elsewhere.

WATCH OUT Customers who don't set up an overdraft arrangement, but allow their current account to slip into the red, could find they are paying an extra 10 per cent or so in interest. So make the arrangements first.

Debit Card

What it is It is a slim line version of your cheque book and cheque guarantee card. Instead of writing a cheque you hand over this card. It will be swiped through a machine and your current account will be debited.

When to use it It is ideal in places like supermarkets where your trolley load of shopping could easily breach the £50 limit on your cheque card, and it is easier to carry than a cheque book and card.

What it costs The card is free but if spending on it pushes you into overdraft, the charges are the same as above.

WATCH OUT Don't jettison your chequebook completely – not everywhere accepts debit cards yet. But they are catching on fast.

TIP · A great advantage of debit cards over cheques comes on your bank statement. The debit card transaction shows the name and address of the shop where it was used, a cheque will only give you a number, leaving you to guess what the amount covers.

Credit Card

What it is A credit card is a plastic card that you use instead of money to pay for goods and services. Every month the total is billed to you and you pay in one go, or by instalments over the coming months or years. It also gives you, free of charge, a certain amount of insurance cover. Each customer has a pre-set spending limit and when that is used up you have to stop using the credit card until you have paid some money in, or until they offer a higher credit limit. If you use your credit card to pay for something worth £100 or more, and the manufacturer or shop goes out of business you will usually have a claim on the credit card company. Some credit cards also give you what is known as purchase cover on goods over £50. That means that if you lose the goods, or they are stolen or damaged, within 100 days or six months (or whatever the limit is on your particular card) of buying, the credit card company will refund the money.

When to use it Credit cards are ideal for putting off payment. Used cleverly (making the big purchases immediately after the statement date) you can have up to six weeks' free credit. Good for purchases of over £50 which is the limit of most cheque guarantee cards, and it saves you the worry of carrying large amounts of cash. Expensive to use if you want to repay the money over a period of longer than six months.

What it costs Credit card interest is charged monthly and it is usually somewhere in the region of two per cent a month. That doesn't sound much but on a yearly interest rate it's quite high. Most cards also charge an annual fee of around £10.

WATCH OUT If you miss the payment deadline, you will be charged interest on the whole amount for what you thought was the interest free period. Unless you are strict with yourself, you will find you spend more with a credit card than if you rely on cash and cheques.

Charge Card

What it is A charge card is like a credit card, except that you have to pay the bill in full every month. Some cards, particularly the ones known as Gold cards, offer an overdraft facility running alongside the card to get round this problem. There are no pre-set spending limits so you can buy a

Rolls Royce providing you can pay the bill when it falls due.

When to use it The overdraft rate is nearly always cheaper than a credit card interest rate, so a charge card that offers one is a better bet for people who want that facility.

What it costs Membership of charge cards, such as American Express and Diners Club, is quite high, and you often have to earn a substantial salary to be allowed to join.

WATCH OUT You may feel that the only extra you get from a charge card is status. If that is the case, it comes expensive.

Store Card

What it is A store card is another type of plastic card. It works in the same way as a credit card, but its use is limited to one chain of stores. It can be known as a charge card (Marks & Spencer call theirs a charge card) but you don't have to pay the bill in full at the end of the month.

When to use it Ideal if you shop a lot in one chain of stores and they don't accept any other credit or charge cards.

What it costs Store cards are free, but the rate of interest charged on outstanding balances can be, and often is, higher than that charged by credit card companies.

WATCH OUT There are two main drawbacks. Firstly, they make you spend more. Store cards are not on offer because they speed up transactions in shops, or because they ease administration. Shoppers are encouraged to take them out because it is a proven fact that they tempt you to spend more. They also limit your choice. If you have a store card you have to shop in that particular shop to use it. You may see the goods cheaper somewhere else, or something that you would prefer to buy. But you can't use your card to make the purchase.

Hire Purchase

What it is HP panders to your worst 'I want it now' impulses. You see something you want, and can't afford. If it comes with its own line of credit – usually described as, say, £5 a month or £2.20 a week, or whatever – you are tempted and you sign up. Sometimes without even asking for how many weeks or months you will be paying.

When to use it As little as possible. HP loans are more expensive than those set up in advance through a bank, and tend to be pricier than paying the balance off on your credit card. They can be useful to people who wouldn't qualify for a bank loan because you don't have to be as financially creditable.

What it costs As HP companies are less strict about who they take on, more of their deals turn out to be bad debts. You, the customer, have to pay for these bad debts so interest rates are higher. Check the APR, and compare it with that offered by say, a bank loan, and you will find that the HP agreement is usually way out in front. Don't be fooled by the cost per week that HP deals are sold on: if the interest rate is not within a stone's throw of the bank, don't sign up.

WATCH OUT The APR has to be quoted. That is the law. If it is not, don't touch the deal. And remember, you don't actually own the goods until you finish paying for them (that is why it is called 'hire' purchase), so if you default, you could lose them. And you won't get your money back either.

Mail Order
What it is Mail Order is simply buying goods from a catalogue. You leaf through until you spot what you want and you send away for it, through a mail order agent. Once you have received it, and you like it, then you pay for it. Either outright, or by spreading the payments over a number of weeks or months.
When to use it A good easy way of buying clothes and household goods, but remember you don't feel the quality. You might find a jacket looks much better on the catalogue model, and is cheaper than a similar one you have seen in a local shop, but when you actually get it, you could find it is made of cheaper and inferior material.
What it costs Nothing. Mail Order companies don't charge interest on the money you owe them. Ten years ago they would have made this back by charging more for the goods, but increased competition and smarter shoppers have stopped this. Prices in catalogues are very competitive nowadays.

WATCH OUT You might be tempted by the glossy pictures to buy too much.

Personal Loan
What it is A personal loan is the posh term for borrowing money from a bank or building society. You tell them how much you want to borrow, and for how long and, if they approve it, they will tell you the rate of interest and the monthly payments. That is a personal loan. Far and away the cheapest and best way to borrow money over one to five years. And it has another distinct advantage over HP agreements. If you default on the payments then, ultimately the bank or building society will confiscate the goods, sell them, take the amount owing to them and give you the rest. For example if

you borrowed £2000 to buy a car and failed to pay off the loan while you still had a further £500 to pay, then the bank would sell the car. If it sold for, say £1500, the bank would take £500 (plus an administration charge) and give you the rest. A similar situation with an HP agreement, would mean that the car would be repossessed and you would be left with nothing.

When to use it Set up a personal loan before going to buy a car, large household goods, furniture and so on. Work out how much you can afford to pay back per month, and make sure the repayments fall at about that level. If they are too high, extend the loan. For example, paying back £1000 over a year at 12.05 per cent interest (that is an APR of 24.7 per cent) would be £93.75 a month, over two years it would be £52 and over five years £27. But remember, the longer the loan, the longer you make the payments so, ultimately, you pay much more for it.

TIP · Make sure the length of the personal loan does not exceed the life of the purchase, otherwise you will still be paying for it long after it has gone. That applies to holidays too. Holiday loans should never be for longer than a year, or you will be needing another holiday before you have paid off the loan on the first.

What it costs The interest rate on a personal loan is usually what is known as a 'flat rate'. That means if the rate is quoted at 10 per cent, you will be paying interest of £10 for every £100 borrowed. The APR is much higher of course. And a good rule of thumb is that the APR on a flat rate loan is usually just under double the rate quoted. So the APR on a 10 per cent flat rate would be around 19 per cent. Once you have taken out the loan, the rate never changes so you know exactly what you have to pay back every month. It is better value when interest rates generally are low, and likely to rise, than when they are high and likely to fall.

WATCH OUT The drawback to a personal loan is that you have to set it up before you make your purchase. It is no good for impulse buying (though to many people this may be an advantage). But once you have it set up, it turns you into a cash buyer which may improve your chances at say, a garage, of negotiating a good discount on a car.

Save and Borrow

What it is This is a bank account you can use to save in and borrow from – hence the name. You choose a savings level, and the bank allows you to borrow up to 30 times that amount. So if you choose to save £20 a month your borrowing level will be £600. The account has its own cheque book, so it is more flexible than a personal loan because you don't have to go into the bank to agree the loan before you buy something, nor do you have to tell the bank what you are buying.

When to use it Good for household purchases that you can't buy outright, and you don't want to buy on HP.

What it costs When you are in the red, the rate of interest will be about the same as that of a personal loan, and if you are in credit then you will get some interest, but not a lot. So if you find you are saving more than you are spending, move your money to a proper savings account.

WATCH OUT Don't be tempted, by this type of account, to overspend. Just because the loan is on offer, you don't have to take it up. As you pay off some of the loan, you can top up your borrowing so it encourages you to spend to your limit. If you think this would lead you astray, don't open a save and borrow account.

Credit Union

What it is A Credit Union is a small non-profit-making bank run by people like yourself. They are taking off fast in this country – mush-rooming in factories, housing estates, offices, clubs, churches. And I highly recommend them.

They work like this. People who work or live together – have what is known as a 'common bond' – get together to set up their own 'bank'. You put in savings of up to £2000 and can borrow up to £4000 very cheaply. Credit Unions are run by their own members, with no interference from outsiders, but they conform to a very definite set of rules. Although the committee will know your financial affairs – how much you have on deposit and how much you have borrowed – they are not allowed to pass on any of this information. Nor can anyone run off with the cash box. Deposits are all insured. So discretion and security are assured.

If there is no Credit Union near you, try getting together with a few friends and setting one up. People like yourself are doing it all round the country and once they are up and running you will wonder how you ever lived without them.

When to use it Credit Unions are ideal for people who might find it hard to get a loan anywhere else. Not necessarily because they are a bad risk but because no one else wants to be bothered with a little loan for say school shoes or Christmas. Others borrow for larger items, such as a car or a holiday.

What it costs Interest on Credit Union loans works out at 1 per cent a month (that is an APR of 12.68 per cent), which is much cheaper than anywhere else. There is virtually no bad debt. Some Credit Unions also offer money counselling to people who have not been very good at budgeting in the past and they have saved many a debtor from an unhappy life. Interest on savings is equally low.

If you do want to start one up in your community or workplace, you will get a lot of help from the Association of British Credit Unions, 48 Maddox Street, London W1R 9BB, or the National Federation of Savings & Cooperative Credit Unions, 1st Floor, Jacob's Well, Bradford, BD1 5RW.

REFUSED CREDIT

No one will lend you money unless they think you can pay it back – with interest. Having an honest face is not seen as any sort of guarantee nowadays. There are more fool-proof methods. The most basic check before being offered, say, instant credit in a store is to ask if you have any credit cards. If you do, that might satisfy the requirements. The next step up is to run your name through a credit reference agency. This is a data base of names and addresses which will show up if you have been a bad debtor in the past, or had any county court judgements against you.

If you are refused credit, ask if a credit reference agency has been used. If it has ask which one, and then ask the credit reference agency if you can see your file. It will cost you £1, and by law, they have to show it to you. If there are mistakes on the file, ask to have them corrected.

The most sophisticated check that is done is what is known as credit scoring. This takes into account your life style and assesses you as a risk. Five main categories are considered – your job, salary, marital status, home, and bank record. So a married man who has been in the same job for 10 years, owns his own house and has a bank account will be a good risk. A single parent in a rented flat with no job and no bank account will be a bad risk.

If you move house a lot, are unemployed and have a county court judgement against you, it is unlikely that you will get much in the way of credit. But you are in good company. I was turned down recently for a credit card because I don't own my own home (it is in my husband's name) and I don't have a job (I am self employed). Yet I consider myself a good risk for a loan. If you think you should qualify and have been turned down unfairly, then write and tell the card company the real score.

GETTING FREE CREDIT

There are times when you can borrow money and pay no interest.
- Credit cards usually offer up to five or six weeks' free credit. Play your

cards right and you can use the plastic to buy for six weeks while leaving your savings in a building society earning interest. Then write a cheque to pay off the credit card.

● Charge cards – which always have to be settled monthly – don't charge interest.

● The offer of 0% interest is a lure to get you to buy. The interest is free, but check that the goods are what you want and are not more expensive than elsewhere.

● Goods on account – some store cards and company accounts give you the goods and you pay by the end of the month.

● Mail Order – no interest is charged in many cases so long as you keep up the payments.

YOUR RIGHTS
Cancelling an Agreement
If you buy a sofa you would not expect the salesman to ring you up a day or two later and say he has changed his mind and sold it to somone else instead. He would be breaking his contract with you. Well, a loan is a contract too. Once you sign on the dotted line, you are committed to the payments. You can't just arbitrarily change your mind. Unless . . . and there are two specific instances when you are entitled to a cooling-off period.

■ You deal face to face with the lender

■ You sign the agreement in your own home (or at least not in his premises)

If both these factors apply then you do have a cooling off period. A day or two after you signed the form, you will be sent a copy of the agreement and you then have five days to change your mind.

The law is very specific about who can cancel. If the wife saw the lender for the first meeting, took the form home to sign, then asked her husband to sign it, then the agreement could not be cancelled. Why? Because the last to sign is deemed to be the one that counts – in this case the husband. He wasn't at the face to face meeting so you don't fulfil the cooling off criteria.

Faults
If the goods are faulty and you get no joy from the company (or it has gone out of business), try the lender. The credit company has as much liability as the shop or garage. But keep making the payments while you try to get the fault put right.

Loan Insurance

The most common loan insurance is on your mortgage – either through an endowment policy or a mortgage protection plan. But you can add insurance to any loan you take out. It will cover you if you are made redundant, fall seriously ill or die.

If you die, the loan will generally be paid off in full by the insurance. Otherwise, if you are ill or made redundant, the monthly payments will be paid for whatever period you chose when you took out the agreement. The longer you want them paid, and the larger the loan, the more expensive is the insurance.

Like all insurance policies you have to weigh up the advantages of having it against the cost to your household budget. And only you can do that.

=================== *Don't get caught out* ===================

• Never lie, or amend the truth, on loan application forms. The credit companies want to lend you the money so if they don't, it is because they really don't think you will be able to afford the repayments. Believe them.

• Don't borrow money unless the APR is quoted. If it is not, then the rate of interest is probably sky high. Go elsewhere.

• Avoid doorstep money lenders. Their trade is illegal, their rates extortionate and their business immoral. Once in, you are caught for life.

• Applying for a new credit card because the old one is up to its limit is foolish and dangerous. Deep in debt is where you will end up.

• Don't act as guarantor on anyone else's loan unless you are prepared to make the payments. That is what you are signing up to do. Many's a friendship that has been ruined by this.

• Keep an eye on payments – check how much you have paid off and how many months there are left to pay. Companies can get it wrong.

• Remember that credit is just another word for debt. There is nothing wrong with saving up first and paying cash.

• If you are spiralling into debt, do something about it fast. Turn to the next chapter, and get reading.

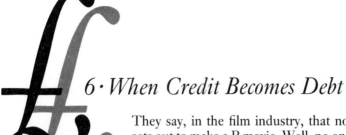

6 · When Credit Becomes Debt

They say, in the film industry, that no one ever sets out to make a B movie. Well, no one ever sets out to get into debt either. Nonetheless, thousands of people skid into serious financial difficulty every year, causing stress and suffering to themselves and their families.

For some, it is simply a case of overspending. Being tempted to buy, buy, buy, knowing, or finding out later that they can't make the payments. But for others it is a crisis that tips them over the brink. A family which has a big mortgage, a couple of credit cards, or maybe they're buying a car and some furniture with a personal loan or on HP, may just be coping financially. Then something hits them: Dad loses his job; or becomes ill and can't work, so there is no overtime coming in; or the parents get divorced; or one of the children ends up in hospital necessitating a lot of extra spending on petrol and visiting or . . .

The list is endless, but what it means is that less money is coming in or more is going out. And that means they can't make the monthly payments. Before they know where they are they have slithered out of credit and into debt.

Sometimes you don't even notice, or don't want to notice. The ostrich factor comes into play, the feeling that if you ignore the warning signs it will go away. It won't. You got yourself into debt, whether deliberately or through no fault of your own, and I am afraid you have to get yourself out of it again. But there is a lot of help available and plenty of people who will be able to give you a helping hand. The awful thing about owing money is that the interest keeps adding on to it. A debt of £1000 left to its own devices will double in seven years. Ignore it for five or six months and it will have increased to £1100. If you couldn't pay it in the first place, you will find it more difficult later on. So the key factor in dealing with debt is to do something quickly. But you won't do anything unless you admit that you have a serious financial problem in the first place. How many of these fit you?

- You don't open letters from the bank
- You pay the minimum on credit and store card bills every month
- You applied for a new credit card because you reached the limit on the old one
- You regularly write cheques that you know will put you into overdraft
- You send the children to your Mum's for a good meal

- You have skipped a payment on the mortgage or rent in the past year
- You are thinking about switching all your loans to one single company where the payments will be lower, but longer

If you answered 'that's me' to three or more you have debt problems. Don't panic, they are not necessarily serious or long term, but you must do something about them now.

A useful rough guide is that if the total that you owe, not counting your mortgage, comes to more than six times your total monthly income, you owe too much and it will take only a tiny push to put you into debt. If your debts stand at three to six times your total monthly income, caution should be your watchword.

Debt problems break down into three main groups:
- Verging
- Short term
- Long term

They all have solutions. You may be having problems at the moment but you can and you will come out the other end. It may not be easy, it may not be simple, it may not be quick but it will happen. So don't give up. You have taken the first positive step by reading this, so you are on your way.

VERGING
People who are verging on having a debt problem are those that constantly think that if they can just stagger through this month, then everything will be OK because next month . . . And next month comes and they say the same thing all over again.

The solution is quite simple – belt tightening. In order to get back in control of your finances you have to spend less for a week, a month, maybe even three months. Once you have got yourself back in shape then budget more carefully and you will be fully financially fit again.

Belt Tightening
Account for everything you spend and cut out all extras. It is only for a short period, but it is crucial that you really do spend less in this period.
- Give up evenings out – whether it is a pint with the lads, an evening at the pictures, meals in town or ten pin bowling, you must be strict with yourself and turn it down.
- Write letters instead of making social phone calls and avoid making any calls before 1.00 pm.
- Don't buy new clothes or shoes, make do with what you have got.

- Watch what you spend at work, or in the shops if you are at home all day. Keep your food simpler to shave your budget. Hide your credit cards from yourself. Don't carry them around and you can't be tempted to use them.

If you can stop yourself putting anything more on your plastic, and you pare the rest of your monthly budget down to the bare essentials you should be able to pay off the balance quite quickly. That will stop large interest payments being added on every month so you move from a vicious to a virtuous circle.

- Take stock of why you overspent in the first place – what leads you astray? Is it plastic cards, too many meals out, buying clothes, a holiday abroad that wrecked your budget, a washing machine that needed replacing, impulse buying, or just plain lack of control of your cash? If you know what it is, then you should be able to solve the problem. Either re-balance your budget to afford, say, two visits to the pub a week. Or cut down on those extras.

TIP · Painstakingly monitoring for a week or two, recording every penny that you spend (see Chapter 3) will give you a reliable guide to your spending pattern. Most people are genuinely surprised at how they spend their money, even where they are apparently effective budgeters. By jotting down what you spend, and where you spend it, you can cut right down in the crucial places.

And here's the other step you must take.

Contingency Fund
Start a Rainy Day account. This is a savings account for emergencies. It works like this. You decide how much you can afford to save every week or month. And be realistic. If you go for too high a figure you will never make the payments. If it is too low it won't ever be large enough to be any use. Once you decide – be it £2, £10, £25 a month – save it regularly. As soon as you get your wage or salary put the money into your RD account. If you leave it to the end of the month, there will be nothing left to save.

Once it is up and running leave it – that money is for emergencies. And make your own rules on this. Be specific about what constitutes an emergency you think worthy of dipping into the fund for. A burst pipe, a prang in your car where you have to pay a £50 excess, a month when there is no overtime, perhaps even Christmas. In the past, those sort of things would have crucified your budget and left you struggling to pay the bills. Now, you can dip into the RD account, and budget with the rest of your money, happy in the knowledge that, at last, you are in control of your cash.

SHORT TERM

Short term money problems are one step further on. They can be helped by a few months' of serious belt tightening, but they often need a bit more. Indeed many people in this category have already cut down or cut out all the extras in their life. Yet they still can't quite get on top of their budgets. Usually, though, they can see a light at the end of the tunnel. If they can get through the next few months, or even the year, then things will get better. Perhaps their training will have finished by that time, or the children will be at school so the wife can take on a part time or full time job, or perhaps the husband is temporarily out of work but should get a new job soon or whatever. In the meantime you can't cope with your debts. Well, here's what you do.

There are two paths you can take here:
- Do It Yourself
- Get the help of a professional money adviser

DIY

If you decide to go it alone, you will be taking much the same steps as a professional debt counsellor would. But you will be doing it on your own. There is no reason, at all, for you not to unravel the problem yourself. So here is how to start. Make yourself a Personal Balance Sheet. That is the posh term for writing down what you have coming in every week and how you spend it.

The trick here is to try and make the income larger than the expenditure. If it is not, can any of these solutions help you out:
- are you entitled to any more DSS benefits?
- is there a wage rise in the pipe-line?
- can you take in a lodger?
- can you, or your partner, get a part-time job?
- can you work more overtime?
- are you entitled to a tax rebate?
- have you the right tax code?

And cut back on the spending anywhere you can (see Chapter 3 for advice on how to do that).

> *TIP* · Check any life insurance or loan insurance you have to see if they cover losing your job or an accident happening. If they do, and it matches your circumstances, make a claim.

Personal Balance Sheet

INCOMINGS	*week/month*	*monthly*
Wages/salary		
Spouse's earnings		
Maintenance		
Pension		
Other		

BENEFITS		
Income support		
Unemployment		
Family Credit		
Child Benefit		
Sickness/invalidity Benefit		
Pension		
Sick Pay		
Maternity Pay		
Widow's Benefit		
Attendance Allowance		
Mobility Allowance		
Invalid Care Allowance		

OUTGOINGS		
Rent/mortgage		
Mortgage endowments		
Community Charge		
Service charge/ground rent		
Pension plans		
Insurance		
Water charges		
Gas		
Electricity		
Coal/oil/calor gas		
Housekeeping		
Food		
Phone		

TV licence/rental	_____	_____
Children	_____	_____
Pets	_____	_____
Birthdays/Christmas	_____	_____
Travel/fares	_____	_____
Car Tax/insurance/MOT	_____	_____
Petrol	_____	_____
Repairs	_____	_____
Clothes	_____	_____
Shoes	_____	_____
House items	_____	_____
Entertainments	_____	_____
Health	_____	_____
Fines	_____	_____
Maintenance Payments	_____	_____
Emergencies	_____	_____
TOTAL	_____	_____
Total income per month	_____	_____
total expenditure per month	_____	_____

Once you have got your spending down, and your income up, then you might have some money to start paying your creditors (these are the companies to whom you owe money). If you don't have a surplus you must get help and advice urgently, before things get out of hand.

The chances are you won't have enough, but many creditors will be at least partly satisfied if you are paying something. What you need, is to get the interest stopped. That way, you will have a chance of paying off the balance.

There are several steps to take:

● cut up your credit and store cards, and send half back to the creditor. If you don't have them, you won't be tempted to use them and by sending half back, your creditor will know that you mean to cut down your spending and not increase his bills

● don't write any unnecessary cheques. That will keep your bank account under control

- write to your creditors. Most of them are well used to dealing with people who get themselves into debt. And they all say one thing: tell us what is happening. If you don't get in touch and explain why you are not paying the bills, they will assume that you are a 'won't pay' rather than a 'can't pay' and treat you accordingly with threatening letters that will eventually lead to court action.

Priority debts

All debts are important, but some are more important than others. These are the priority debts. If you don't pay them, they have ways of making you know about it. So make sure you take them seriously and act quickly if you fall behind. Either pay up, if you can, or go and get professional debt counselling advice.

Debt	What could happen
mortgage/rent	you could lose your home
community charge	bailiffs or sheriff officers will sell some of your household goods to pay the bill or you could be imprisoned (in England or Wales), or the money can be deducted from your wages or benefit or your bank account frozen.
water, gas, electricity	supply cut off
unpaid magistrates court fine	imprisonment
HP	repossession of the goods

Few of these steps can be taken without court action of some sort, though your water, gas and electricity can be cut off, and HP goods repossessed if you have paid less than a third of the price. For the others there is a strict course of action that has to be taken. And it will be. Ultimately you will be at the receiving end of a court order if you don't take any action. So do something. It is never too early or too late to contact the lender and try to work out some repayment schedule.

TIP · Creditors can repossess goods that are bought on HP if you fail to make the payments. But many credit agreements are not pure HP agreements. Check your agreement. Only if it says Hire Purchase or Conditional Sale, can the goods be repossessed.

Dealing with creditors
You must write to them and enclose four things.
- a letter explaining your circumstances
- a copy of your Personal Balance Sheet
- a Plan of Action to pay off the debt
- half of the credit or store card.

The letter will tell them who you are, outline why you are having problems, suggest to them what you are going to do about it and ask for the interest on the debt to be stopped. If you like you can adapt the letter below.

The Personal Balance Sheet (p. 47/48) you will already have drawn up. Make a copy for each of your creditors and keep one for yourself.

The plan of action tells the creditor how much you think you can afford to pay every month. It could look something like the one opposite.

━━━━━ *Letter to Creditors* ━━━━━

Address
date

Dear Sir,

Account number and your name

I am writing to you in connection with the above account on which I owe £___.

I am being made redundant at the end of this month. I will receive no redundancy payment, because I have only been with the firm for 18 months. My wife has a job as a shop assistant and will try to do more overtime, but we will have to survive on a very much reduced income. After paying for all the household essentials there is very little left over at the end of the month.

However, I intend to do my utmost to clear the above debt. As you can see from the enclosed personal balance sheet and Plan of Action I should be able to cope with paying off the sum at £___ per month. However, unless you can consider suspending interest charges, it will be impossible for me ever to clear the debt.

I have enclosed half my store card to you, so no new purchases will be added to the above sum.

I am writing to all my other creditors asking them to accept a similar arrangement and, in the meantime, I will be trying to find another job. Although I am 47, I am a skilled toolmaker so I hope to work again.

I shall keep you informed of all developments.

Yours faithfully,

Enclosed: Personal Balance Sheet
            Plan of Action
            Half my store card

From Alison Mitchell

Monthly income	£500
Monthly outgoings	£425
Excess	£75

Current debt	monthly repayments
High Street store card	£35
Credit card	£27
HP payments (credit or credit sale agreements)	£16
	£9
Personal loan	£25
Total per month	£112

£75 is 67 per cent of £112 so I anticipate reducing all of my payments by a third, on a pro rata basis as follows:

Suggested schedule of repayments

	original	new
Store card	£35	£23.50
credit card	£27	£18
HP payments	£16	£10.75
	£9	£6
personal loan	£25	£17

Most creditors will accept this sort of plan because if the debt comes to court, then the interest will be stopped to allow the debtor to pay. They are just doing it one step earlier. It is crucial now not to miss a payment. If your schedule has been accepted and is realistic and you make the payments, on time, every month you are on the way to complete recovery.

Should something happen that stops you making the payments – you lose your job, become ill – then you must write immediately to the creditors telling them what has happened and suggesting a new plan of action. If you don't, and you miss a payment, they will fall heavily onto you.

Even if you do want to go it alone, there is no harm in getting a bit of guidance. Try the National Debtline on 021 359 8501. They are specialists in the self-help approach and can give general and specific help on the whole self-counselling process.

TIP · Some creditors are distinctly grouchy upon the initial approach. This does not mean they will not eventually reach a rational compromise with you. A mixture of grovelling and common-sense explanation can work wonders. Persistence, that's the name of the game.

Getting Professional Help

If you don't feel up to taking on your creditors yourself, there is plenty of professional help available. Citizens' Advice Bureaux should be your first port of call. Nowadays many of the larger offices have professional money advice counsellors attached to them who will be able to steer you through the above steps. And letters to creditors on CAB-headed notepaper can carry more clout. Or ask at your local town hall to see if there is a debt advisory service linked to the council. Even ring the Samaritans – they will put you onto a counsellor. But do something. Your doctor, your minister, your priest, your librarian, even your neighbour may know who would be the best person to help you.

TIP · There are around 1700 charities in this country with a total of £86 million to give away every year. You may qualify for help from one of them. Perhaps you, or one of your family is ex-service, or you worked for a large company with a benevolent fund or someone in your family is suffering from a specific disease, or your local round table or the Salvation Army could help. To find out more, get hold of a copy of *A Guide to Grants for Individuals in Need* (Available from the Directory of Social Change, Radius Works, Back Lane, London NW3 1HL). It is a costly £12.95, but DSS offices, some CABs and libraries have it.

LONG TERM

Long term debt problems are a whole different ball game. They need more radical solutions. Belt-tightening won't work here. But you are by no means a hopeless case. There are steps you can take to get you out of the debt mire. It will take longer, it will be emotionally more distressing, but you will make it.

A serious debt problem usually stems from a combination of three things – a lack of surplus income; a number of priority debts such as the Community Charge; and the sheer scale of other debts. The average debt clinic client owes around £16 000.

The reason your problem is more serious than a short term debt problem has nothing to do with what you owe. It is not the size of the sum, it is the inability to pay which makes it worse. Perhaps you are in your 50s and have just been made redundant. Getting another job will be very difficult. Or you may be a single parent with your youngest child only months old, so you won't be in a position to go out to work for another five to six years. Or you are a pensioner, or have a serious illness.

In all of these cases increasing your income to a level where you can pay off your debts is going to be difficult. And I strongly recommend that you don't try to go it alone. Get the help of someone who knows what they are doing. Along to your local Citizens' Advice Bureau with you.

Debt Counsellors

There are debt counsellors and CAB offices in most city centres. They offer advice and help on financial and emotional family problems – from how to organise a funeral to working out which benefits you qualify for. Their advice is free and confidential, so don't worry about anyone else knowing the state of your financial affairs.

But most of all – you won't shock them. However serious your affairs are, no matter the number of debts, or the amounts, they have seen it all before. There is nothing that you have done that will faze them. Don't put off going, the longer you leave it, the fewer are the options open to you.

Dealing with the Debt

A professional debt counsellor or experienced money adviser will start by listening to your problems – even something as simple as that will prove to be a tremendous relief to you. The next step will be to deal with any immediate crisis. It is often the threat of the gas or electricity being cut off, or receiving a summons that prompts you to go alone to the CAB in the first place. So they will help you to sort that out. You will then go on to fill in a questionnaire which will be turned into a Personal Balance Sheet. Your counsellor will check, from this sheet, whether or not you can claim any more DSS benefits and whether you are on the correct ones. He or she will also check that you are not paying too much, or too little, tax.

They will then work out the scale of your problem and explain your options to you. It may be that they can see a way to follow the path described above: of writing to your creditors, getting the interest stopped and coming up with a payments schedule that you can keep to. If that is not going to solve your problem, the next step in England and Wales might be to apply for an Administration Order. (There is no such thing as an Administration Order in Scotland.)

Administration Orders

This is a system of using the court to help you to clear your debt (by administering it) and keeping your creditors at bay. First you have to qualify for one. To do that, you need to fulfil three criteria:
- your total debts amount to under £5000
- you have more than one debt
- you already have a county court judgement against you

Go along to your county court and ask for a form, or your local CAB might keep a stock. The form is called 'N 92 An Administration Order Application'. The court officers will know what you want if you describe it. Debt is a growth business and you will find they know the ropes and are very sympathetic.

Take the form home and fill it in. It is not difficult, but it is time consuming. You will have to list all your debts and also give an accurate account of the money you have coming in every week or month, and the outgoings you need to live. If you have a Personal Balance Sheet already drawn up, use it for all these details. But, be honest.

Then it's back to the court to 'swear it in'. That's much easier than it sounds, too. You just have to read the words off a card, swearing that what you wrote on the form is accurate. The Court Officer will also often ask for proof of the debts so take your latest bank or credit card statements with you just in case. The court will then write to all the creditors you listed on the form asking if the details you gave are correct and about six weeks later you return to the court for the hearing.

It is nothing like *Rumpole of the Bailey* or *Perry Mason*. The District Judge who officiates, hears the case 'in chambers', that means in a small office, so no one else knows about it. Occasionally a representative of some or all of your creditors may be present. The District Judge then decides how much you can afford to pay to your creditors every month. And, most importantly, the interest is stopped. So you only pay back the amount outstanding. And it can be a very low amount – around £4 a month is standard if you are unemployed.

And that's it. Every month you pay the set amount into court and they send it on to the creditors. If you can't pay, let the court know the reason and if it is sound and understandable they will allow you to miss. If your financial circumstances change – perhaps you or your spouse have lost their job – then you can go back and get the payments reduced. But if you don't pay because you spent the money on something else for no real reason, you will be in serious trouble because you will then be in breach of a court order.

In some circumstances, perhaps if you are a single parent, you can apply for what is called 'composition'. That means that you can ask the court to write-off a certain amount of the debt and pay back the rest. This would really only apply to people who had absolutely no hope of ever repaying the money they owe, but they are becoming more common. Check with your local debt counselling advisers. Not for nothing are Administration Orders known as 'poor man's bankruptcy'.

At the moment Administration Orders only cover debts of less than £5000, but there is legislation currently going through parliament which could change all this. It is likely that the limit could be raised to £50 000, and a time limit on how long you pay the debt for. This will make an Administration Order a better step than opting for bankruptcy.

The downside of an Administration Order is that you cannot get any more credit while you are paying off your debt. To many people with money problems, this is seen as a plus factor. If you currently have, say, credit and store card debts of more than £5000 that you can't pay, your creditors will eventually take you to court. Much the same thing will happen, that is the interest will be stopped and monthly repayments set.

Bankruptcy/Sequestration

There is one final step that you can take: to file for bankruptcy, or sequestration as it's known in Scotland. This is not something to do lightly. You may lose your debts when you become a bankrupt, but you lose everything you own of any value as well. And the emotional stress is enormous.

Bankruptcy Filing for bankruptcy in England has a Catch 22 feel to it. You file because you have no money, but you have to pay a fee of £130 in order to file. Any assets you have, such as a home, car, furniture, television, will be sold and the money used to pay off some of your debts.

Bankruptcy is not given automatically just because you ask for it. If your assets amount to over £2000, the Receiver could opt instead for an

Individual Voluntary Arrangement where he does much the same as a professional debt counsellor would, that is add up your income, deduct the outgoings, and share what is left among your creditors on a pro rata basis. The Receiver will not order any payment from income. Mortgage and rent arrears are not written off by bankruptcy.

Even when you are discharged – probably after two years – you can't apply for any more credit without disclosing that you are a discharged bankrupt.

It's worth getting hold of, and reading thoroughly, a good little booklet called *Insolvency Act 1986 – A Guide to Bankruptcy Law*, available from the Insolvency Service, 2–14 Bunhill Row, London EC1Y 8LL. It's clear and informative and you should read it carefully before petitioning.

Sequestration If you have debts of over £750 in Scotland, you can apply for your own bankruptcy by the trust deed method. You go to a solicitor or a chartered accountant and sign a trust deed. The courts are then asked to declare you bankrupt and a trustee is appointed. Some interim trustees and lawyers will charge you, some will not, so ask if they do. All your financial affairs will be handed over to the trustee, generally the insolvency practitioner from the firm of chartered accountants first approached. During this time you won't be able to apply for credit of over £250 without disclosing that you are an undischarged bankrupt at which point your loan will almost certainly be turned down. With credit of under £250, you don't have to say you are an undischarged bankrupt. Normally you will be discharged after three years. Exceptionally it could be longer, or less in some circumstances, particularly for old age pensioners.

Don't think that bankruptcy or sequestration is an easy solution to overspending, it's a very serious step that could cost you your home and any other assets.

Although it takes the immediate pressure off, it will paralyse you financially for life. You will probably never be able to get a mortgage, or credit or even an HP agreement again. And credit and store card companies will not want to take you on. For young people, it is virtually a financial life sentence. Explore every other avenue first, and see a CAB or money advice centre counsellor.

Consolidation Loans
Have you ever wished you could pay off all your loans and end up paying less per month! Seen it advertised in the papers and been tempted? Well, stop right there. Consolidation loans, as they are called, are bad news.

They work like this: you have several loans – a couple of store cards, perhaps, that you are building up borrowings on, maybe two or three HP payments to meet each month and a credit card on which you have reached the limit. You are hard pushed to meet your payments every month and you see the advert. What is on offer is one large loan which will pay off all your debts so that you make one large repayment every month. The real sweetener is that the one large repayment is smaller than all the little ones put together.

Magic? No, you are just changing short term debts for long term ones. You pay less per month because you are paying for a lot more months. Imagine your debts were £3500 in total. Assuming you had intended paying back the loan over three years, you would have monthly bills of £125 and a total to pay back of £4500. At the same rates of interest, a ten-year consolidation loan would cut your monthly payment to £61 but increase the total that you repay to a massive £7300. And if you had trouble with your borrowings before, a consolidation loan will compound it. As soon as you reduce your monthly payments, as sure as eggs is eggs, you will take on another loan. So you end up with a large long term debt and another short term one.

If the consolidation loan is secured on your home, and you can't make the payments, you will end up losing it. Now that is not something that could happen for failing to pay your credit or store card bill. So steer clear of these offers.

Keep an Eye on the Kids

No, it is not drugs or alcohol or smoking I am warning you about – but debt. Kids growing up today have never really known what it is like to save first and then spend. They come from a generation that is tempted by Instant Credit, Easy Money, have it now, pay for it later. So what chance have they to come to terms with saving first and then going out to buy. They might buy a stereo today, on HP, want a new one with more knobs in six months' time and buy it, despite the fact that they haven't paid off the first one yet. Selling it on to a friend for £50, won't do much good.

Once you reach the age of 18, you are legally responsible for your own debts. That means, in simple terms, you're allowed to borrow money. So, if you have children over the age of 18, ask them if they know how much debt they have. Chances are they won't have a clue. So get them to make a list, add it all up and check that the bills come within their budget – be it wages from work, paper rounds or just pocket money. Because unless they know where they are, they will never be in control of their cash. And if they are not in control, they could be in debt. If their debt problem looks serious, take some of the steps outlined earlier, or get them along to a debt counsellor.

> *TIP* · For credit read debt. Every time you see a sign offering 'Easy credit' or 'Instant credit', just remember it is not credit they are offering. It is debt. Translate it in your mind and ask yourself: do I want to take on this debt? If the answer is no, then don't make the purchase.

Jean's Story

To end on a positive note, let me tell you about Jean.

Born in Cowcaddens in Glasgow, Jean never had much money. She married young, her husband left her and she drifted into debt. From not being able to pay the HP instalments, Jean slithered all the way down to borrowing from loan sharks. She came on *Bazaar* to tell her story – of how she was so frightened that she hid behind the sofa so that the heavies collecting the loans couldn't see her.

But she got lucky. She told a friend her problem and that friend took her along to the local Credit Union. The committee there agreed to help. They took over all her loans which by now totalled £2400 and paid them for her. She was put on a payments schedule to repay the money to the Credit Union.

She not only did that, but continued to make the payments, which turned into deposits once the loan was paid off. Her life has been transformed now that she has had some money counselling. She saves up through the Credit Union or borrows only what she can afford to repay so there is no more worry over loan sharks and bailiffs. Now she is all set to go away on holiday for the first time in her life. If Jean could do it, what is stopping you?

7 · Simple Savings

Saving money can be one of the most boring occupations around. Most of us would prefer to be out spending it, or using the money to top up the family budget every week.

Don't give in to the temptation – for a savings account is the adult equivalent of a child's security blanket. With a bit of money behind you, you will have the financial confidence to complain if the services on offer are not up to scratch; you will cope with unexpected bills and crisis payments and you will be able to afford treats – from holidays to new clothes. Best of all, you won't be constantly worrying that an unexpected bill might be just around the corner, and panicking when it arrives. The cushion of a savings account allows you the breathing space to cope. And that's worth a lot to most of us.

Why Save?

Saving money is an insurance policy for the future. You may be putting cash aside in case something unexpected crops up, or to bolster your pension when you retire, or for something specific such as a new stereo or next year's holiday. Whatever the reason, make sure you know what it is. Because unless you have an 'investment aim' you won't know what sort of savings account to go for. And everyone should try to save something. If you have an income at all, try to set aside a little to build up a nest egg.

All the time that money is in a bank, building society or National Savings account, interest is being added. If the balance is low, it won't be much but every little bit helps. And when you need the cash, for whatever reason, it will be a little more than you expected. It will also save you a lot. If you have to borrow money in an emergency you have to pay interest on it and that will set you back further.

Take this example:

Mrs Smith decides to save £10 a week.	
At the end of six months she has saved	£260
Interest at 10 per cent has been added	£ 13
So her total is	£273
Her washing machine breaks down and the replacement cost is	£273
She takes the money out of her savings account, pays the bill and continues saving so that, six months later,	
at the end of Year One her balance is	£273

Mrs Brown also needs a new washing machine and she borrows £270 to pay for it.

The rate of interest is a flat rate of 12 per cent, paid back over one year. At a cost per month of £25.19.

For a whole year she has paid a lot more than £10 a week, but has nothing to show for it at the end.

How to Save

No matter how good your resolution, saving can be difficult. That is because there are so many other pockets for money to go in. By the time you've got through the month there is nothing left for the savings account. So you hope next month will be better and you will save double. But next month is exactly the same and you don't save again.

The answer is to save first. As soon as you get your wages or salary, switch the savings into another account. That way, if you get to the end of the month and there is nothing left, something else will have to give. So it may help you to curb your impulse buying as well.

How much you save every month is up to you. If you are saving for the holiday of a lifetime in Australia you will probably have a greater incentive to put more away than if you are just hedging your bets against a rainy day in the future. But be realistic. If you set the figure too high, either you won't make the payments, or the cost to the rest of the month's budget will be tediously high. And if you don't save enough, there won't be anything in the kitty when you need it. Whatever figure you opt for – be it £10 a month, £15, £25 or even £50 – make sure you do it regularly. In good months and in bad. You will be surprised how quickly it grows.

The Contenders for Your Cash

There is only one type of account that suits rainy day cash. That is a simple deposit account with a bank, building society or the National Savings. It is easy to put the money in, take it out again and there is no risk whatsoever to the sum. When you go to get it, it will all be there along with a slice of interest. If you opt for a building society they will lend your money on to people wanting to buy their own home; if you opt for a bank you will be lending on a wider range of loans; while at the National Savings you are lending your money to the Government.

Not that any of that should influence your savings choice in any way. Like everyone else, go for the account that offers most interest on your money.

Interest
The interest rate you get depends on two main factors:
- how much money you've got
- how long you can afford to tie up your cash

How much The more you have, the more interest you will get is the general rule. Some accounts offer the same rate, regardless of whether you have £1 deposited or £10 000. That is OK if you don't have much money, but if you do then you should look for a better deal. Try an account which offers a high rate on large sums, or go for a tiered account. This is the sort of account where the rate of interest rises as you pass a known level. Perhaps you'll get

5.5 per cent on balances of up to £500
7.5 per cent on balances of up to £1000
9.5 per cent on balances of up to £5000
10 per cent on balances over £5000

It is ideal for savers who don't know how much they will have in the account, or who use the account a lot so the balance goes up and down regularly. When they are flush they will get a good rate of interest, when they are not they will get less.

How long The longer you can tie your money up, the more interest you will get. Accounts which offer instant access pay less interest than accounts where you have to give seven days' notice or 30 day's notice or even 90 days' notice. If you know you won't be touching your emergency fund, you could move it to a seven day account and get a bit more interest. This has the added advantage of stopping you using it for an impulse buy because you have to wait seven days for the money.

I think the long notice accounts of 90 days and upwards are more suited to pensioners who perhaps have a larger nest egg to tuck away, and see it as an income producer rather than money they are actually intending to spend. Anyone having one of these accounts really must have an ordinary savings account too, with a bit of money in, that they can use for everyday bills and spending.

WATCH OUT Careful of the small print on some of these accounts – although you may be able to get instant access on a 90-day account, you will lose 90 days' interest on the money. And that could be quite a loss.

How interest is paid Generally, interest is paid monthly, quarterly, six-monthly or annually and it can be added to your account, transferred to another account or sent to you by cheque. The more frequently the interest is paid, the lower it tends to be.

Interest will be paid net or gross:
Net – this means that tax has been deducted before it is paid.
Gross – this means that tax has not been deducted and it is your responsibility to pay it if you are a tax-payer.

There is another set of letters which you should know, and that is CAR – the Compounded Annual Rate. This is the rate you use to compare interest rates. Check the CAR on an account paying monthly and that on an account paying interest annually, and you will see that you get a better rate on the latter, even though the rate quoted on the bank or building society poster may be the same.

Interest can be variable, fixed or with a guaranteed premium.

• variable – this simply means that the rate of interest will move up and down with the interest rates in general. When you hear a news report on 'bad news for home owners' (which means mortgage rates are going up) that is good news for savers because savings rates will be increasing.

• fixed – very few savings accounts have their interest rate fixed, that is non-moving. The only ones that do also fix the number of years when they will keep the rate at that level, and it will normally be called a bond. You could get say, a two year fixed bond. That would not only fix the savings rate for two years, but it would tie your money in for that time.

> *TIP* · Fixed rate bonds are a good deal when rates generally are going down and a bad deal when they are going up.

• guaranteed premium – this is a fudged fixed account. To attract money into high interest accounts the bank or building society will sometimes offer to guarantee the differential. So if the account starts out paying say five per cent over the share account rate, it will continue to pay five per cent more whether rates move up or down. That guaranteed premium or differential is usually set for the first few years of the life of the account, not indefinitely.

Risk
Putting your money into a bank or building society or National Savings account is taking no risk with it at all. If you lost your money in an account like that, it would mean that the financial system as we know it, is in such

chaos that your money would probably be worthless anyway. You would be pushing it around in a wheel barrow and worrying less about how much it was worth as to whether you could still afford a loaf of bread.

However, should a building society get into difficulty, you are guaranteed to get back 90 per cent of the first £20000 of your savings. If a husband and wife have a joint account, you will get 90 per cent of £40000. With a bank, you'll only get back 75 per cent of the first £20000.

National Savings accounts are backed by the Government.

Savings and Tax

Who pays If you are a tax payer then you will have to pay tax on any savings interest you get – at your highest rate. That means 25 per cent if you are an ordinary tax payer, 40 per cent if your a high rate payer. If you are not a tax payer, then you don't have to pay tax on your savings. So make sure that you are not.

How tax is collected Tax is automatically deducted from all bank and building society accounts at the rate of 25 per cent. So ordinary rate tax payers don't have any problem here.

National Savings accounts are a hybrid – some deduct tax at 25 per cent, others don't take tax off at all, so if you are a tax payer you have to declare the interest on your tax form, and some accounts are not liable for tax and are known as tax-free.

High rate tax payers They have to make up the difference by declaring the interest on their tax form. The Inland Revenue will charge them 40 per cent tax on the interest, deduct the 25 per cent already paid, and send them a bill (or change the next year's tax code).

Non-tax payers They must tell the bank or building society of their financial status (that is, non-tax payers). They should fill in an exemption form that the branch will have and the interest on any savings will be paid tax free. That means they will get a quarter more interest on their money.

If you don't fill in the appropriate form, you will lose 25 per cent tax just like everyone else.

If you sign an exemption form in good faith, and find out later in the tax year that you have become a tax payer – perhaps you got a job – tell the bank or building society immediately. It is your responsibility and you will be breaking the law if you don't.

Husband and Wife

If a couple conform to the traditional family of husband out to work, wife at home looking after the kids, they should do some tax planning. It is very simple and will save them pounds. All you do is put the savings into the wife's name. A wife, like everyone else, has a personal tax free allowance. If she isn't earning (or not earning enough to breach that allowance) then it makes financial sense to have the savings in her name because she can offset the interest against her tax free allowance – and get a quarter more in interest. On savings of £2000 she would make around £50 a year more in interest.

Pensioners
Anyone of 65 or over with an annual income of more than £13 000 should read this section. It is a little complicated, but it could save you quite a lot of cash.

Once you pass your 65th birthday (whether you are a man or woman) you qualify for what is known as the Age Allowance. This is a larger personal allowance than younger people get. If you are a married couple, then the Married Couple's Allowance also goes up as soon as one partner is 65 (and it doesn't matter which it is). These allowances go up again at age 75.

This increased allowance is designed to help older people on a reduced income, by allowing them to pay less tax. However, if you are wealthy you don't get it. The Government deems 'wealthy' as exceeding an income limit set by them. In the 1991–2 tax year that limit was £13 500.

The problem is that everyone over 65 automatically gets the age allowance, so 'wealthy' pensioners have it taken back again. It is done by cutting £1 off your age allowance for every £2 of income you have over the income limit. And it feels like you are paying tax at 50 per cent.

If you are a borderline case, a bit of judicious juggling with your money may save you from this swingeing penalty. For example you might be able to move some of your money into National Savings certificates where interest is tax free, or into gilts (see page 80) where you could go for a capital gain rather than income. However, don't risk your capital with anything dodgy just to save a few pounds in tax.

8 · What's On Offer

Bank and building society customers are spoilt for choice when it comes to savings accounts. There is a product for you – regardless of what you want out of the account: good rates of interest, easy access, monthly interest, no tax deducted from the interest, a chequebook and interest, regular savings . . .

The problem comes in trying to identify which one it is. So, let's start by going through the basic types of accounts that are on offer.

BUILDING SOCIETIES
Instant Access
What it is An instant access account allows you to put money in and take it out again without penalty. You often get a plastic card with it which, along with your PIN number, allows you to use the ATM machine. So you have 24-hour-a-day, seven-days-a-week access to your money (providing there is cash in the machine when you get there!). These accounts often offer a tiered rate of interest so the more you put in the better is the rate of interest.

When to use it Ideal as a working account on which you make a lot of transactions: putting any extra money in that you have, and getting easy withdrawals when you need the cash out again.

Drawback Not the best rate of interest around.

Fixed Rate
What it is This account, often known as a bond, pays a rate of interest that is fixed for a certain number of years.

When to use it Go for this account if you want to tie your cash up. Ideal if interest rates are high and likely to fall, not so good when rates are low and likely to rise.

Drawback Difficult to get your money out during the life of the bond, without paying an interest penalty.

Guaranteed Differential
What it is This account starts life offering a better return than the normal building society rate, say 5 per cent. And guarantees to keep that gap no matter what happens to rates. This guarantee is usually set for a number of years.

When to use it If it would help your budget to know the rate of interest you

get, but you don't want to tie yourself into a bond for one or two years, this is a good half-way house.
Drawback Usually you need a lump sum to start the account off, and the differential won't be held indefinitely.

Monthly Income
What it is This type of account pays the interest monthly. You put in a lump sum, usually at least £1000, and the interest will be sent to you or credited to another of your accounts on a set date every month. The interest will vary with rates in general.
When to use it If you have a nest egg saved and don't want to dip into it, but your income is too low for you to live on. Ideal for pensioners who don't want to spend their lump sum, but can't live on their pension.
Drawback The interest rate is lower than it would be in an account paying half yearly or yearly interest.

High Rate
What it is An account that pays a better rate of interest than you would get elsewhere.
When to use it If you have a large lump sum you want to put on deposit.
Drawback You need a large lump sum to qualify. There are a welter of minimum deposit and length of notice conditions on the different accounts, so choose the one that suits you best.

Regular Savings
What it is This account is for people wanting to save the same amount every month.
When to use it If you need the discipline of a pass book to encourage you to save, then this is for you.
Drawback Not readily available nowadays, and not a particularly high rate of interest. These accounts can also have a lot of conditions attached, such as what and when you can withdraw, topping up with extra savings, and penalties on missing payments.

SAYE
What it is A Save As You Earn account for saving regularly for either five or seven years. All building societies offer the same terms, but you can only have one account. You choose how much you want to save from £1 a month to £20. At the end of five years, a bonus equivalent to 14 monthly payments are added. If you leave the capital and the bonus for another two years, you will get another 14 months' bonus added. You can miss up to six

monthly payments, provided you make them up at the end and if you stop the scheme, after the first year, you will get interest of around 6 per cent on the money. Stop during the first year, and all you get is your money back.

When to use it Good for people wanting to save regularly who can do so for five or seven years. Could be an ideal way to save up the deposit on your first home, if you start early enough. Often run in tandem with company share option schemes.

Drawback Not a good rate of interest if you stop the scheme in the middle, and five years is quite a long commitment.

Current Account

What it is Runs like a bank cheque account, offering interest on deposits. Charges interest on overdrafts, and gives the usual current account services on an ATM card, cheque guarantee card, facilities for standing orders, direct debits, electronic transfers and overdrafts. Some savings accounts offer the facility of a chequebook to make withdrawals easier, but these don't usually offer any other extras.

When to use it If you need a current account, this is a good alternative to a bank current account for most people.

Drawback Not always quite so financially sophisticated as those run by banks. For example, cheques can take longer to clear.

BANKS

Most High Street banks run many of the accounts outlined above. They may vary in the small print but the principles will be the same.

The banks also offer a few additions, though you may find that some building societies also offer these types of accounts. The difference between banks and building societies grows narrower by the year.

Seven Day Account

What it is It is a deposit account on which you have to give seven days' notice of withdrawals, or lose seven days' interest.

When to use it If you want a bank deposit account offering a low minimum balance, then this is it.

Drawback The rate of interest can be very low on these accounts, so check before you open one.

Money Market

What it is This is a top rate account, paying the highest rate of interest available. It gets its name because the money you invest in the bank is re-invested directly into the money markets – it is a professionals' game and pays very good interest. Of course, you won't get this on deposits of £100. You have to be a big player to get these rates – probably investing over £25 000 to get the real top rate. And the rates will move up and down all the time.

When to use it If you have a very large sum of money that you want to put on deposit.

Drawback Not available to many savers because of the size of deposit you need.

High Interest Cheque Account

What it is It is a hybrid, combining good savings interest with a cheque account, but not offering the full service on either. You need a larger minimum deposit than the normal £1 needed to open a cheque account – upwards of £1000 usually. On that you get a good high rate of interest. In return, you limit the services you will get. A cheque book will be on offer, but you can usually only write large cheques, say £250 or more, and/or the number of cheques you write in a year will be limited. Or you may have to pay a management charge.

When to use it If you are saving up for things like holidays, Christmas or even school fees, this account is ideal. You get the high rate of interest on your money and the convenience of being able to write a cheque on it. You would need an ordinary current account for the rest of your money affairs.

Drawback If it is the highest rate of interest that you are looking for, choose a savings account that does not offer a cheque book.

TESSA

No it is not the name of the Chancellor's wife – it is a new type of savings account that was introduced a few Budgets ago. It should be a must for your long term savings, if you are a tax payer. The initials stand for Tax Exempt Special Savings Account, and that is what it is. It is a savings account, with special rules, which pays interest tax free. Anyone over 18 can have one – and only one – and they are available from banks and building societies. The fine print and charges of each scheme are different, but the general rules are the same.

A TESSA works like this:

- it is a five year account
- you can pay in a total of £9000 (though this figure may be increased in future Budgets), with up to £3000 going in in the first year, and £1800 for the next four years.
- interest that is added on to the account is tax free.

- if you withdraw the interest, you will have to pay tax on it.
- if you withdraw more than the interest the account will be closed.

Banks and building societies which run the schemes set the rate of interest on their own scheme, though they have to be competitive otherwise no one would opt for their TESSA. However, watch out for the extras: charges, penalties for switching to a TESSA with another bank or building society, or the need to set up a 'feeder' account to transfer money to the TESSA. As a rule of thumb, the TESSAs offering the highest rate of interest, will have the most catch clauses in their small print.

NATIONAL SAVINGS

Investing in National Savings is, in fact, lending money to the Government. So it is very safe. You run the accounts either by post or through Post Offices. The accounts vary considerably in what they offer, so there is probably one that is ideally suited to you and your financial circumstances.

Investment Account

What it is This is a savings account which pays interest gross (that is without deducting tax from the interest). The rate of interest is generally quite high, though in line with other savings accounts.

When to use it If you are a non-tax payer and want a good rainy day account, this could be it.

Drawback You have to give a month's notice of any withdrawals, though there are no interest penalties.

Ordinary Account

What it is A savings account offering a very lowly rate of interest. The first £70 of interest is tax exempt, thereafter it is taxed at whatever rate you pay. The rate of interest is two-tiered. To earn the higher rate, you have to keep the account open for a whole calendar year, and in the months when you have over £500 in the account you will get the higher rate. In the months when it is under £500 you get the lower rate. If the balance is over £500 for the whole year, you will get the higher rate for the whole year.

When to use it If you are a high rate tax payer keep enough in the account to get £70 of interest.

Drawback The rates of interest are low, and the conditions complicated. Interest is only paid on money that is in for a full calendar month. So be certain you make deposits at the end of a month and withdrawals at the beginning.

Savings Certificates

What it is This is a scheme which offers a fixed rate of interest exempt of tax. You buy the current issue of savings certificates, hold them for five years, and get back your money plus the interest. Interest works on a sliding scale: you get much less in the first few years, and most in the final year. So unless you think you can hold for the full five years, don't buy them. Index-linked Savings Certificates work on the same principle, but the rate of interest is not fixed. It is the equivalent of the rate of inflation. So if inflation is running at seven per cent a year, that is the rate of interest you will get. On top of that there is an additional rate of interest that is guaranteed, and not linked to inflation at all. It rises from a lowly rate in year one to a more respectable one in year five.

When to use it It is ideal for locking your money away for five years, if you are a tax payer. The rate of interest is quite high because you don't pay tax on it.

Drawback Not good for non-tax payers – they can do better in a building society or bank, or in Capital Bonds if you want a five-year investment. The rate of interest is disappointing if you have to withdraw money in the early years.

> *TIP* · National Savings now use the word tax-exempt when they mean that no tax is ever paid. Tax free means you pay tax, if you are a tax payer. So tax payers, and particularly high rate tax payers, do better out of tax-exempt schemes.

Income Bond

What it is The minimum investment in this account is £2000 and what makes it special is that the interest is paid monthly, into a bank or building society account of your choice. No tax is deducted, but tax payers will have to declare the interest to the Inland Revenue and pay tax on it.

When to use it Ideal for non-tax payers wanting to use their capital to supplement their income.

Drawback You have to give three months' notice for withdrawals.

Capital Bonds

What it is A little like savings certificates, except that the interest is paid gross. Ideal for non-taxpayers who don't want income from their money. You deposit your cash, and five years later you get it back with the interest added in full. If you are a tax payer you will then have to declare that interest to the Inland Revenue, and pay tax on it every year. The rate of interest is fixed, so you know exactly what you will be getting.

When to use it If you are a non-tax payer with savings of over £100 that you want to tie up for five years, this one is for you.
Drawback If you withdraw early, the rate of interest is low.

SAYE
What it is A regular savings plan that runs alongside an employee share option scheme.
When to use it If you are saving to buy shares in the company you work for, under an approved Inland Revenue scheme.
Drawback Not available to everyone.

Yearly Plan
What it is A regular savings plan that pays interest tax free. You save between £20 and £200 a month for 12 months, then leave the money in the account for a further four years. You get a guaranteed rate of return, which pays out the largest rate of interest in the fourth year. If you want to continue to save regularly, take out another Yearly Plan at the end of the first year.
When to use it Ideal for tax payers wanting to save regularly.
Drawback You get a low rate of interest if you have to withdraw money in the early years.

Children's Bonus Bond
What it is This is a recent National Savings innovation, looking to attract children's money. It is a five-year hold, with a rate of interest paid annually, and a bonus added at the end if you hold for the full five years. You can buy the bond in £25 chunks. It was launched with a rate of interest of 5 per cent a year, with a bonus of 47.36 per cent being added if you hold for the full five years.
When to use it Ideal for money given to the children from parents. At the moment, Inland Revenue rules discourage parents from giving children money that will produce more than £100 of income a year. This account gets round that rule because it is tax exempt.
Drawback Children, who are generally non-tax payers, will get a higher rate of interest in a bank or building society savings account where they can now get their interest gross. The maximum investment is £1000.

Premium Bonds
What it is You invest your money in a prize draw. Three months after you deposit your cash, your money is eligible for the draw. Ernie chooses numbers at random and if yours comes up you will get between £50 and

£250 000. Every £1 you put in, gets a number, so you think that you have a lot of chances of winning. In fact the chances of you winning the jackpot are one in 1.9 billion and the chances of winning any prize with one number are one in 11 000, but people do win every month.

When to use it Worth tucking £100 into Premium Bonds – after all you might just win.

Drawback You get no rate of interest on the money so if you don't win, all you get back is your initial investment. If you are over 16 you have to buy Premium Bonds in tranches of £100, if you are under 16 then the minimum purchase is £10, but someone has to buy them for you.

TIP · Should you want to invest less than £100, you can make your £100 purchase, then cash in up to £95!

FRIENDLY SOCIETIES

These are a relic of the last century when people used them to save for their own burials. If it is tax efficiency you want, ignore them at your peril. Investing with a Friendly Society is at least a ten-year hold. You put in a lump sum, or agree to an annual premium. The money is invested in ultra safe havens and at the end of the term you get the money and the profit back, with no tax deducted. Because of their tax efficiency, there is a Government limit on how much you can put in, currently £200 a year or £18 a month. And you can only have one account.

If you have to break the contract in the first seven-and-a-half years, you will be lucky to get your gross premiums back. Thereafter, up to the life of the policy, you should get more. Don't open one of these accounts if you don't think you can support it for the ten years, but if you do want one of these accounts, look for the ads in the financial pages of your newspaper.

HOW TO CHOOSE

You can't choose an account until you know what you want from your money. And you may not necessarily want the same thing from all your money. For example you may be prepared to tie up some of it for a year, or even five years, but keep a portion of it in an instant access account. Make sure you know exactly what you want from your money before you choose the account and make the investment.

Remember, this chapter is only dealing with that portion of your savings which is the bottom chunk – the part that you want to take no risk with at all. If you are prepared to take a bit of a risk with any of your money, read on to Chapter 9.

You are a non-Tax payer

Can you tie up your money for 5 years? _____

YES ▶ *Capital bond*

NO ▼

_____ Can you tie up your money for 2 years? _____

   YES ▶ *Fixed rate bond*

   NO ▼

_____ Can you tie up your money for one month? _____

      YES ▶ *Investment account*

      NO ▼

_____ Do you want a monthly income? _____

         YES ▶ *Bank or Building Society monthly income account*

         NO ▼

_____ Do you need to know the rate of interest? _____

           YES ▶ *Guaranteed differential*

           NO ▼

_____ Do you want a regular savings plan? _____

              YES ▶ *SAYE or Building Society regular savings plan*

              NO ▼

_____ Do you have a large lump sum? _____

                YES ▶ *High rate*

                NO ▼

_____ Is there a little of the gambler in you?

                  YES ▶ *Premium Bonds*

You are a Tax payer

Can you tie up your money for 5 years or more? _____
YES ▶ *Savings certificates; Friendly Society*
NO ▼

____ Can you tie up your money for 2 years? _____
YES ▶ *Fixed rate bond*
NO ▼

_____ You are able to give no notice _____
YES ▶ *Instant access*
NO ▼

_____ Do you need to know the interest rate? _____
YES ▶ *Guaranteed differential*
NO ▼

_____ Do you want a monthly income? _____
YES ▶ *Bank or Building Society monthly income account*
NO ▼

_____ Do you want a regular savings plan? _____
YES ▶ *SAYE; Yearly plan; Building Society regular savings plan; Friendly Society*
NO ▼

_____ Do your savings fluctuate a lot? _____
YES ▶ *Tiered account*
NO ▼

_____ Do you have a large lump sum? ___
YES ▶ *High rate; money market; TESSA*
NO ▼

_____ Is there a little of the gambler in you?
YES ▶ *Premium Bonds*

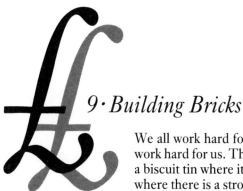

9 · Building Bricks

We all work hard for our money, so we want it to work hard for us. There is no point in keeping it in a biscuit tin where it won't make any interest, and where there is a strong chance of it getting stolen. No, investing it is the key.

As I outlined in the last chapter, there are plenty of safe havens for your cash if safety and security are the key requirement. And there is nothing wrong with that. Never feel you ought to move out of a bank, building society or National Savings account and into something riskier. Plenty of fairly wealthy people keep large sums of money in a savings account because they know that they will get a good rate of interest on it and that there is no chance of them losing any of the capital.

For others, taking a bit of risk can mean getting a better return on their money. As the old saying goes, 'You have to speculate to accumulate.' But when, and how, do you improve the chances of making a better return on your money?

WHEN TO MOVE ON

If you can say yes to the Magnificent Seven questions, you should start thinking about moving on from simple savings to something more sophisticated. If you have even one 'no', stay where you are in the meantime.

1 *Have you enough money coming in every month for the household budget?* Yes ☐ No ☐
By that I mean can you pay all your bills, cope with your mortgage or rent, keep your financial balance when an unexpected demand lands on your doormat and still have a little left to save every month.

2 *Have you an emergency fund?* Yes ☐ No ☐
This should be large enough to save you from worrying about unexpected bills and in an account where you don't touch it needlessly.

3 *Have you a pension?* Yes ☐ No ☐
Everyone who works should make provision for their retirement – relying on the state old age pension will not make for a very happy time after you give up work. Your company may have a scheme you could join (or are already in). That is the best option for most people because the company makes a contribution to it. Failing that you should have your own Personal

Pension Plan – and this must come before you think about taking any risk with your capital.

4 *Have you adequate insurance cover?*   Yes ☐   No ☐
The problem with insurance is that you could spend everything you earn on it – to cover the house, the car, your life, your holiday, your health, your pets, your mortgage, even your contact lenses. But you have to draw the line somewhere. Start with the basics and make sure your house, mortgage and car are fully covered and if you have dependants, you must make sure you have adequate life insurance too. After that, it is up to you what you insure, but if you feel you need insurance on something, go for that before you start out on riskier investments.

5 *Have you a buffer fund?*   Yes ☐   No ☐
A buffer fund is the next step up from a rainy day account. By the time you are thinking of investing in things that can seriously damage your wealth you will be splitting up your money into sections – one of which you will take a risk with. But below that should come a high rate savings account. That is the buffer that will stop you being financially wiped out if you lose what you risk.

6 *Are you sure there's nothing looming?*   Yes ☐   No ☐
There should be no dark clouds on your horizon. If you think that there could be a big bill to pay in the near future – perhaps the car is going to need a lot of work doing on it, or the house might need reroofing, or you are thinking of moving, or redundancy could be on the cards – then don't think about risking any money you might need for that. Next step investment is longer term, not for dipping in and out of, so wait till the sky is blue again.

7 *Can you afford to lose this money?*   Yes ☐   No ☐
This is the crucial question, because it sums up risk. If you can't afford, or wouldn't like, to lose your investment – don't make it. The chances are that you won't lose the money, or at least not all of it, but you could. So take the decision now and if it would scupper you financially, or psychologically, then leave the money in the building society.

SO YOU ARE READY TO MOVE ON
What you want from your money, though you may not know the technical term for it, is capital growth. You want the money you have now to be worth as much in the years to come, or more. If your lump sum is large enough to

be able to buy a sizeable family car, or put in a new kitchen now, then you want it to be able to buy at least that in the years to come. At the very least, the capital growth should beat inflation. Hopefully, it will do much better.

If you leave your money in a savings account you will get interest added to it every year. You know the rate of interest, so you know that at the end of the year, your money will be there plus the interest. If you leave the interest in the account, rolling up, you will find that your money will roughly double every seven years or so.

With investment for capital growth there are no such general rules. Your money will probably be invested, in some way, in shares. Shares can, and do, go up and down so at times you will be doing very well, at times very badly. That is the risk you take, but you can spread that risk. The more you spread the risk, the less likely you are to make a runaway gain with your capital. But unless you are super wealthy, I don't recommend that you take the full risk of buying shares yourself.

THE OPTIONS
PEPs
Personal Equity Plans were launched by Nigel Lawson in his 1986 Budget, but they have been streamlined and simplified since then. Because of the tax advances, they are ideal for tax payers. A PEP is a fund of your own money that you use to buy shares, but it is managed by a professional fund manager. You pay no tax on any dividends from the shares in the fund, and no tax on the gain you make when the profits come out. There are limits on how much you can put in per year – currently £9000 per person – and on the shares you buy. They come in all shapes and forms: regular savings PEPs; lump sum; unit trust; investment trust; PEPs linked to your mortgage or to school fees. Look around and choose the one that suits you best.

WATCH OUT PEP management charges can be high so ask the fund managers what they charge before you sign up, or you could see a good part of your profits going to them.

Share Option Scheme
These are plans which offer you shares in the company you work for, or its parent company. Generally it will be quoted on the stock market, and the schemes have to be agreed by the Inland Revenue. They work like this: the company agrees to set aside shares for employees at the current price, or up to 20 per cent less. You then save through a SAYE scheme for five or seven years, getting all the bonuses you are entitled to. At the end of that

time, you have the choice of using that money to buy the shares, or just keeping the money. What it means is that if your company's shares have gone up, you will buy them, if not you won't. So it is a no-lose situation. Once the shares are yours you can keep them, sell them, give them away – it is up to you. You don't pay income tax on the shares when you get them, but you will be liable for Capital Gains Tax if the profits breach the CGT level, currently £5500. You might think that if you make that level of profit, you wouldn't mind paying a bit of tax on the rest (see p. 90).

Unit Trusts

Investing in a unit trust is often seen as a half-way house between a savings account and buying shares yourself. A unit trust is a pool of investors' money that is managed professionally, and it allows you to spread your risk.

Imagine you had £1000 to invest in shares. The chances are you would spread it between one or two shares, three at the most. Now, if any one of these shares does badly, it will probably wipe out any gains you make on the others. Invest instead in a unit trust, along with money invested by thousands of others, and you spread the risk of one share doing badly. The fund manager will buy perhaps 500 shares or 1000 and you have a minute part of each share, so one or two bombers won't affect you too much. Of course, one or two high flyers won't push your investment up so dramatically either.

There are many types of unit trusts: general funds investing in a mix of UK shares and looking for balanced steady growth; growth funds; recovery funds; funds that invest in specific areas such as the Far East or Europe or America or oil funds; gold funds; even green funds if ecology is your pigeon.

The more specialist the fund, the higher the risk but the higher the potential reward. For example, if you choose an oil fund you will do well if the price of oil goes up, and badly if it goes down. You could also go for a cash unit trust or even a gilt fund.

WATCH OUT The management charges on unit trusts are high. An initial charge of five per cent and an annual charge of between one and two per cent, so that means that the price of your units has to go up by over seven per cent for you to start making a profit.

Don't buy unit trusts, and expect to see a quick profit on your money. Expect to leave them alone for up to three years, but keep an eye on them. If they suddenly rocket in price, think about taking your profit. To buy units, you can cut coupons in newspapers and magazines, deal with the company direct, or go through a stockbroker or bank or building society that deals in shares.

If you want more information on unit trusts write to the Unit Trust Association, 65 Kingsway, London WC2B 6TD. Tel: 071 831 0898.

Investment Trusts
These trusts are rather like unit trusts. They pool investors' money and buy a spread of shares or gilts and the investor has a share of the investments. But they differ in several ways. Unit trusts are open ended, which means the more people that invest, the larger the fund becomes and the more money the fund manager has to invest. Investment trusts are launched and closed once a certain financial target has been reached, and that is the size that the investment trust will stay.

To invest in one, you have to buy shares from someone else. So investment trust shares are quoted on the Stock Exchange in their own right just like any other company, but instead of making widgets the company makes investments.

To buy shares in an investment trust, you will have to go through a stockbroker, bank or building society that deals in shares. Or you could use one of the investment trust companies' regular savings plans if you want to put your money in on a regular basis. If you want more information on investment trusts, write to the Association of Investment Trust Companies, Park House, 16 Finsbury Circus, London EC2M 7JJ. Tel: 071 588 5347.

Privatisation Schemes
Over the past 10 years, the Conservative Government has sold off, or privatised, many of the previously nationalised industries: British Telecom, British Gas, the electricity companies, the water authorities, and so on. On the back of these share sales, millions of people have become share holders for the first time and made good profits along the way.

Government sell-offs are a very easy way to buy shares. You get a huge advertising campaign telling you what is coming up and suggesting that you register for a prospectus by phoning a special number. When it comes to you, you just fill in a very simple form, attach your cheque, and with luck you are a share holder. There are no buying costs, apart from the price of the shares. You learn about costs when it comes to selling, but even then the blow can be cushioned by a special £15 deal often on offer from the smaller, out-of-London brokers.

The shares are usually priced towards the bottom end of expectations, so investors can often get a good little profit out of the deal. If you see a privatisation in the offing, at least register. Then watch the financial pages of your newspaper to see if they recommend that you pitch in. Follow the advice.

Buying Shares

This is not something I would recommend for the first-time investor. Stick with unit and investment trusts, and even Government sell-offs until you get the hang of how the stock market works. When you are ready there is nothing to stop you investing in shares for yourself. Of course, you will need a middle man, either a stockbroker (look under 'S' in your local Yellow Pages) or a bank or building society that offers a share dealing service. They all charge for buying and selling shares for you, some more than others. Many banks will add a percentage onto the brokers' charge to cover their administration costs, so cut them out and deal with the broker yourself. Choose a 'country' broker, that is one that is based outside London, and you should find the minimum charges within your price range. They can vary from £15 all the way up to £50 from the large London brokers who don't really want the business of small investors. Selling is slightly cheaper, but overall buying and selling charges can work out at 10 per cent of the value of the shares.

The rub comes in choosing the shares to buy. We all want the ones that are going to go up – but which are they? You might have a hunch or go for a company in a sector that is doing well, or just stick a pin in a list. But remember that shares can, and do, fall as sharply as they rise. So if you can't accept that – don't invest.

Most shares pay a dividend twice a year, it is a little like interest and it depends on the number of shares you have. If you work out what the dividend is as a percentage of the price you paid for the shares that will give you the yield, and the yield is equivalent to the rate of interest. For example, a dividend of 10p on a share you paid £1 for, gives you a yield of 10 per cent. So if you want income from your money, with the hope of capital gain thrown in, go for a share with a high yield.

Gilts

When you buy gilts – or gilt edged securities as they are really termed – you lend money to the Government. That won't stop you getting your fingers burnt if you read the market wrongly, but at least the underlying asset will always be there. Gilts are a little complicated to understand, but it is worth persevering as you can make money out of them. And they can be an ideal investment for people such as pensioners wanting a guaranteed capital growth. Gilts are IOUs from the Government. They take your money in chunks of £100 and guarantee to repay it on a certain day in the future. In the meantime they will pay a rate of interest on it. It is that simple. What makes it more interesting is that you can buy and sell gilts just like shares. So the buying and selling price of £100 of gilts is seldom £100. If the gilt was launched when interest rates were high and they have fallen, a lot of people will want that gilt so it will cost more than £100. If it has a low rate of interest people won't want it and it will cost less than £100. To get a guaranteed capital growth you look for a gilt selling for under £100, say £92, and hold it until the Government redeems it for £100 and you have a gain of £8. Meanwhile, if the price went above £100, you could take your profit.

You can buy gilts through a stockbroker, or much more cheaply through what is known as the National Savings Register. This means buying them by post through the National Savings. It cuts costs dramatically. Typically it would be around £4 for £1000-worth of gilts. For further details of how to buy, and which gilts are on the register get a leaflet at your nearest main Post Office.

What to Avoid
Never be taken in by adverts that suggest a much better rate of return than you would get elsewhere. If their promise was a guarantee then we would all be investing there. And if it is not a guarantee, then they might as well promise you the moon. Many is the investor who has come unstuck by believing advisers that promise a better return on their money – with no additional risk.

Don't attempt to put money into commodities, penny shares, traded options, vintage cars, alternative investments or any other flavour of the month investment. These are markets best left to the professionals.

Choosing a Professional Money Adviser
There is only one person who really has your financial interest at heart – and that's you. So try to do as much of the ground work yourself as possible. You may still need a lot of help with understanding systems, but if you have a little knowledge yourself you will be able to ask the right questions and you won't have the wool pulled over your eyes.

Financial Advisers
There are two types of financial advisers now, and they have to tell you at the outset which they are.
Independent financial advisers They can sell products from any company and have to get you the best deal around.

One-company salesmen They deal for one company and can only sell you products from that company.

They all earn a good part of their living from commission so that you won't be charged a fee, but do make sure that what they are selling you is the right product for you, and not just a good fee booster for them.

Make sure that whoever you deal with is beyond reproach. Check, before you start, that your adviser is registered. He or she should work for a company that is on the SIB Register. Ask the adviser, or check it yourself. Your local library should have a copy of the register, or you can check it on Prestel. If membership is pending or about to come through or . . . go elsewhere. Because that means they are not a full member so you won't be covered.

And remember, a BMW in the drive and a suite of offices in the posh part of town are not alternative credentials.

10 · Understanding Your Tax

For nearly two centuries we have been a nation of tax payers. Income tax was introduced as a temporary measure in 1799 to fund the war against Napoleon – and it has been with us ever since. It is a tax that is raised by the Government to pay for the running of the country. It funds parliament, the law, the NHS, our defence, part of our council bills and so on. No one likes paying it, but if we didn't the fabric of the country would disintegrate. And it is not just income tax – there is Capital Gains Tax, Inheritance Tax, Corporation Tax, Stamp Duty, and VAT.

We don't need to understand how they all work, but it is worthwhile at least scratching the surface to make sure that you are paying your due, but not personally over-funding the Inland Revenue.

INCOME TAX

Income tax is that awful sum of money that takes your monthly salary down from what you would like to receive, to an amount that doesn't seem enough to keep a church mouse in cheese. Everyone in this country – man, woman and child – is liable for tax. Only the Queen is exempted. What takes people out of the tax bracket is having an income that is too low to trigger a tax rate. We all have what is known as a personal tax allowance. That is the amount you can earn in a tax year before starting to pay tax. If you don't earn enough to reach that level, you don't pay tax.

Tax Free Allowances

If you are single and under 65 you get the
Personal Tax allowance   £3295

Married couples get an additional
Married Couple's allowance   £1720

Single parents with at least one child also get an
Additional Personal allowance   £1720

Widows get an extra allowance for the year they are widowed and the next year they get
Widow's Bereavement Allowance   £1720

Blind people get
Blind Person's Relief   £1080

Older people get additional allowances if they have an income below
£13500 (1991–2 figure) (see page 64 for more details)
Personal Allowance (age 65–74)   £4020
Personal Allowance (age 75 and over)   £4180
Married Couple's allowance (age 65–74)   £2355
Married Couple's allowance (age 75 and over)   £2395

(All these figures are for the 1991–2 tax year. The allowances are
increased in the Budget every year)

If your income falls below that allowance then you don't pay tax. Once it
breaches your level, you start paying tax at 25 per cent and you continue to
do that until your income reaches the next level up when you start to pay at
40 per cent. The 40 per cent level is officially £23000 in the 1991–2 tax
year, but on to that you add your personal allowance or allowances and any
pension contributions you make before you start to pay the higher rate.

And that's it. Under the current Inland Revenue rules 40 per cent is as
high as it goes. Though once you pay at that level, you feel it is high
enough. Sadly, the system isn't quite as simple as that. There is one other
concept you have to take on board in order to check that you are paying the
correct amount of tax every month. And that is the tax code.

Tax Code

If you work for an employer you will pay tax under what is known as PAYE
– Pay As You Earn. It means tax will be deducted every month by your
employer and sent on to the Revenue. In order to know how much to take
off, your employer will use your tax code. The code, usually a series of up
to three numbers and a letter, tells him, or her, how much tax to deduct.

It starts with your personal allowance – whichever one that is – adds on
anything you are liable to tax on, deducts anything you are due a rebate on
and divides the result by 10. Actually it is simpler than it sounds!

Your tax code comes from a Notice of Coding which will be sent to you
in January or February, though you don't always get one every year. Check
that it is correct. It is easy to do if you can crack the code, so here is how to
do it:

First of all the letter. The code ends with a letter such as L or H or P or
NT or whatever. Your Notice of Coding letter should also contain a leaflet
detailing what they mean. So check that yours is correct.

The figures are equally easy to follow. The notice will show what
allowances you have, such as personal, married couples, any regular
contributions you make to charities, and what deductions you have to pay

tax on such as car, petrol, maybe unpaid tax from an account that pays interest gross. The deductions will be taken from the additions and the final figure will be divided by 10. If you are a married man with a company car the sum could look like this:

Allowances		*Deductions*	
personal	£3295	Benefits (car)	£2400
married couple's	£1720	Benefits (fuel)	£ 750
		unpaid tax	£ 172
total	£5015	total	£3322

Allowances set against pay £1693 (£5015 − £3322 = £1693)
Tax code   169H

Tax Year
The tax year in this country runs from 6 April one year until 5 April the next. So the 1992–3 tax year is, in fact, 6 April 1992 until 5 April 1993.

Avoid or Evade
Avoiding tax is human nature. A bit of judicious tax planning should ensure that we all pay as little as we can. Evading tax is illegal. Not declaring your full income, or hiding your savings in an account that you don't tell the Inland Revenue about, is against the law. You will be fined by the IR when you are caught, or perhaps even sent to jail.

Tax Free Income
You don't pay tax on everything. Some income is tax free – and that income falls into four main categories:
- gifts from friends and relatives
- some social security benefits
- certain investments that you make
- prizes and winnings

Gifts Don't look a gift horse in the mouth. If anyone gives you money, you are unlikely to have to pay any tax on it. However, if you start to earn interest on it then that interest will, of course, come into your taxable income.

Social security benefits Some benefits are tax free, others you pay tax on. In general the following ones don't fall into the taxable income category: Sickness Benefit; Invalidity Pension; Attendance Allowance; Mobility Allowance; Severe Disablement Allowance; War Pensions; Industrial Injuries Benefits; Widow's Payment; Income Support; Community Charge Benefit; Housing Benefit and Guardian's Allowance.

Investments Some National Savings products were the first of the tax-free investments to be commonly used. Savings Certificates, and Index-linked Savings Certificates and the first £70 in interest on an Ordinary account are all tax free. As are Personal Equity Plans and TESSAs, though there is a limit to how much you can invest.

Prizes You don't have to pay income tax on any prizes or winnings you get from football pools, casinos, racing, slot machines, bingo, Premium Bonds or the church bazaar. But once you invest the money, any income it produces is taxable.

PAYE

If you are an employee you will pay your income tax under the system known as PAYE – Pay As You Earn. It means that it is your employer's duty to work out how much you should be paying in tax, and deduct it from your wages. He, or she, uses your tax code and a book of quite complicated tax tables to do the sums every month – nowadays usually with the help of a computer. It would be difficult for you to work out whether or not the figures are correct, but if your tax code is correct, the chances are that the right amount of tax is being deducted. If, however, you have a second job, earn money from a hobby, let out a room to a lodger, have interest on money that is not taxed or have income from any other source it is *your* duty to declare it.

Write and tell the Inland Revenue about it. You will find that, if you make a profit from, say, your hobby there are deductions you can make from the total profit to cover your costs, so you won't have to pay too much tax on the profit. If you don't tell the tax man and he finds out about it – and in this computer age, he will – then he will come down on you like a ton of bricks. And you might not find the allowances so generous then. You will also be charged interest on the tax owing and perhaps even fined.

Schedule D

Self-employed people don't come under the umbrella of PAYE. They are taxed under what is known as Schedule D. It means that they don't pay tax on money as they earn it, but in a later year. And the problems start, as many one-hit pop stars have found to their cost, if they spend all their income and have nothing left to pay the tax man. If you are self employed, it is probably worthwhile relying on a tax accountant to sort out your tax for you. You could do it yourself, but the time and effort involved might be too great. You could probably spend your time more profitably on your business and pay a specialist to work out how to minimise your tax bill. His, or her, bill will also be tax deductible.

GETTING HELP FROM THE REVENUE

There is one source of tax help that is easily available and free, and it comes from the tax man himself. All Inland Revenue PAYE offices have a selection of easy-to-read, free and useful brochures, and they cover every tax subject imaginable.

So if you have a problem, ring up (under 'I' for Inland Revenue in the telephone directory), outline what you want and they will no doubt send you the booklet.

There are specialists there to answer your problems in person, or by phone, but they tend only to answer what you ask. They might not volunteer additional information, so the booklets are more helpful for general problems.

Tax and Marriage

If you are getting married solely to reduce your tax bill, do it after the start of the tax year but before 6 May. If there are other considerations, it really doesn't make a pennyworth of difference when you marry.

You will both have, before and after marriage, a personal tax free allowance of your own. This will be unchanged by the exchange of vows. After you tie the knot, the husband will also get the married couple's allowance. If you marry before 6 May, he will get the whole thing. Otherwise he will get it on a pro rata basis – a twelfth for every month you are married in the tax year. If the husband can't use the whole married couple's allowance, the balance can be transferred to the wife. Personal allowances are not transferable.

> *TIP* · An unmarried man claiming the Additional Personal Allowance has a choice in the year he marries. He can claim either the Additional Personal Allowance or the Married Couple's Allowance in that year, but not both. It is the same amount, but the Married Couple's Allowance is reduced month by month, the Additional Personal Allowance is not – so if he marries after 6 May, he should stick with the Additional Personal Allowance. A woman continues to get the Additional Personal Allowance, if she is entitled to it, in the year she marries, thereafter neither of them gets it.

Couples that lived together before they married, and had tax relief on a £60000 mortgage, will lose half of that on the day they marry. A couple (indeed even an unmarried couple nowadays) only qualify for tax relief on a mortgage of up to £30000. If they both have mortgages on separate properties, then they will continue to get the tax relief for a year after the wedding, sometimes longer, if they can show that they are having difficulty selling the property.

TAX AND PENSIONERS

Many pensioners seem to think that they stop paying tax the day they retire. Wrong. They may become non-tax payers because they no longer have a large enough income to take them into the tax bracket, but they are still potential tax payers and if their income rises, they have to pay like the rest of us. At age 65, they do qualify for the Age Allowance, and at age 75 for the higher Age Allowances . How it works, and how to make the best use of it, is explained in detail on page 64.

Pensioners who don't pay tax, should make sure they are not paying tax on any interest they get on their savings. If the cash is in a bank or building society account, sign an exemption form (available from your branch) so that interest is paid gross.

Health care If you are over 60 and have a private health insurance policy, you will get the premiums tax free. Policies which don't qualify are those that offer a cash sum if you have treatment under the NHS. If you are not sure whether yours qualifies, ask your insurer for advice.

Even non-tax payers benefit because the tax is deducted at source (like the MIRAS mortgage scheme) so the premiums go down by 25 per cent. If you are a high rate tax payer you get 40 per cent relief, but the additional chunk is returned to you through your tax code. Providing the recipient of the policy is over 60, the tax relief goes to the payer regardless of age. So if you are lucky enough to have a son or daughter or friend who will pay the premiums, they will get the relief at whatever rate they pay tax.

TAX AND SOCIAL SECURITY

Some DSS benefits are taxable, others are not and it is a minefield working out which is which. Indeed with some benefits like Income Support and Unemployment Benefit, bits are taxable and bits aren't. However, remember that even if a benefit is taxable you only pay tax on it once you pass your personal allowance level.

If you are in doubt, ask your DSS office, your local tax office or the CAB. Don't just ignore it and hope that no one will notice. Paying £1 a week in tax as you get the money is a lot easier than trying to come up with a lump sum to pay off a tax debt in later months.

'PIN' MONEY

If you have any extra income which is not taxed under PAYE, you must tell your local tax office. It might come from running a mail order catalogue, renting out a caravan, giving music lessons in the evening, working in a bar, making curtains, or whatever. Just write a simple letter telling the tax man how much you earned in the past year, what your expenses were and what the profit was. That might be enough, otherwise he will send you a tax form, or ask for fuller accounts. In either case, do what he asks and pay up. It is simpler and cheaper in the long run.

You should also tell the Department of Social Security. If you are earning more than £52 a week, that is the lower earnings limit, you will have to start paying National Insurance. It is not much and worthwhile doing because you will be building up an entitlement to a State pension for yourself.

OFFICE PERKS

Company cars, canteen meals, an interest free loan for a season ticket, free private medical insurance: they can all be inducements, over and above a salary, to make you want to work for a company. Fringe benefits they may be, but if you earn more than £8500 a year you will have to pay tax on the value of the perk.

If you earn less than £8500 a year, in most cases you can have all the perks your employer wants to give you, and pay no tax on them at all. Unless . . .

The value of the perks will be added to your salary and if that then exceeds £8500 you will be taxed on all the fringe benefits. So have a care if you are a borderline case.

INCOME TAX AND SAVINGS

If you have any savings in a bank, building society or National Savings account, and you are a tax payer, you pay tax on the interest. Ordinary rate tax payers, with money in bank or building society accounts pay the tax automatically. If they have money in a NS account, or any other type, which pays interest gross (that is without deducting tax first) they must declare it to the Inland Revenue and they will be billed for it, or have their tax code changed the following year.

High-rate tax payers must declare all their savings accounts and interest to the Revenue and they will be charged the difference between the 25 per cent they have already paid, and the 40 per cent they are due. Any other type of unearned income, as it is known, such as dividends are also taxed at your top rate. Most are taxed automatically at 25 per cent. If you are a high-rate payer you must make up the difference, if you are a non-tax payer you can get a form allowing you to reclaim the tax.

CAPITAL GAINS TAX

You start paying Capital Gains Tax (or CGT) once your profits from things like share deals, reach £5500 in a tax year. That figure is sometimes raised or lowered in the Budget. For most people CGT is an irrelevant tax.

You do not pay CGT on the sale of your home, but you do pay it on the sale of a second home. CGT is levied at whatever rate of tax you pay, either 25 per cent or 40 per cent, though in practice most people who pay CGT are 40 per cent tax payers, and if you think you may have to pay it on something, then get professional advice.

INHERITANCE TAX

Inheritance Tax is not a tax you pay, it is one that is paid by your heirs. But since it is your hard-earned money that will be going to the Government instead of to your family or friends, it is worth doing something about it while you live and breathe. Put another way, of course, it could be the money that should come to you from your parents, but is diverted to the Inland Revenue instead, because they did no tax planning!

Inheritance Tax has to be paid if your estate is worth more than £140000 when you die. That is the 1991–2 figure and it rises, more or less, in line with inflation, every year. You may not think that your estate, that is all that you own, could ever be worth so much, but if you own your own home you could well be closer to that figure than you think.

All money that passes between a husband and wife is Inheritance Tax free. So, if you die and leave everything to your husband (or vice versa), no tax will be due. But when he dies, then his estate will have to be valued and Inheritance Tax paid if it comes to over £140000.

But there are two main ways to minimise the bill:

- Tax plan your will
- Give away money now

Tax Planning in Your Will

Leaving everything to your spouse is a certain way to avoid Inheritance Tax, but when your other half follows you to the great golf course in the sky, then the Inland Revenue could clean up on your money. So make use of the Inheritance Tax allowance. The first £140000 of your estate is tax free so start to pass some of that tax-free part down a generation.

For example, imagine you are very rich. Your house and assets are worth £200000 and you leave all the money to your wife. You die. She gets £200000, and there is no Inheritance Tax bill. Then she dies and leaves everything to your two children. They get £140000 tax free, but have to pay an Inheritance Tax bill on £60000 at 40 per cent. Total bill: £24000.

Now, let's try again.

You are still worth £200000. But when you die you leave £70000 to your children and everything else to your wife – that's £130000. No Inheritance Tax to pay. She dies and leaves her £130000 to the children – again no Inheritance Tax to pay. Total bill: £00000. So £24000 is saved, with very little effort.

Giving Away Money

There are two main systems for giving away money

- making the gifts and living for seven years
- annual and special gifts

Seven-year rule You can't avoid paying tax by just giving away all your money. If you give away an amount that totals more than the level of the Inheritance Tax allowance, then you must live for seven years to ensure no tax is paid on the money. However, no one can guarantee to add seven years to their life. If you die in between times, a percentage of the tax is paid.

Die within	3 years and	100 per cent of the tax is due
	3–4 years	80 per cent of the tax is due
	4–5 years	60 per cent of the tax is due
	5–6 years	40 per cent of the tax is due
	6–7 years	20 per cent of the tax is due

Annual and special gifts You can give up to £3000 a year to anyone or split it among several people (and go back one tax year if you didn't give away money last year); or as many gifts of under £250 as you like providing it is to different people; or certain wedding gifts; or gifts to proper UK political parties or charities; or money that is part of a divorce settlement; you can even support a widowed mother-in-law. But if your Inheritance Tax planning has reached this level, you should get some professional help. A solicitor or accountant will be able to advise you, or get hold of the Inland Revenue booklet, *IHT 1 Inheritance Tax*.

VAT

Value Added Tax is levied on all goods and most services. The usual rate is 17.5 per cent, but on some things like children's clothes, some foods and newspapers the rate is zero. Which means you don't pay it.

If you set up in business you must register for VAT when your annual turnover tops £35000 a year. Thereafter you must charge customers VAT at 17.5 per cent.

This level goes up most years so if you are a borderline case, and will lose work by charging your customers the extra 17.5% VAT, it may pay you to turn down business in the last few weeks of your financial year. You needn't lose the custom altogether, just ask them to wait into your new financial year.

11 · Buying Your First Home

In boom times, owning your own home is as sound an investment as you can have. But in less prosperous times, a home of your own can become a mill-stone that may break you financially. Young couples who bought their dream home for more than they could afford in the late 1980s and then saw interest rates rise to record levels, rued the day they ever put money into bricks and mortar. By contrast, a decade earlier, a couple who made the same financial sacrifice to buy a place of their own would have watched the value of their home double and treble as house prices ran up, uncontrolled.

More and more people nowadays buy instead of rent. Almost two-thirds of the population own their own home, with or without the help of a bank or building society. There are two main reasons for this. It is more difficult to rent a place than it was a generation or so ago, either from the council, or from a private landlord. And by buying your own place, you get something back for all the thousands of pounds you put in. You might find that the monthly cost of a mortgage is similar to what you would pay in rent, but after 25 years the house is yours. With rented property you have to hand it back. It is no foregone conclusion that you will last the course. With properties so expensive now, many people take on a house or flat they can't afford and end up repossessed. And a lot worse off than they had been.

So, should you rent or buy?

RENT OR BUY?

When it comes to making a choice between renting and buying there is usually more than just pure financial considerations to be taken into account. You might want to build up a property nest egg for your old age, or like to feel the security of a home behind you, or perhaps want to have something to pass on to the children. But you must still do your sums carefully before you move into a home of your own.

Owning a house		*Renting a house*	
Mortgage	_____	Rent	_____
Water Rates	_____	Water Rates	_____
House Insurance	_____		
Repairs	_____		
Total	=========	Total	=========

Owning a flat		*Renting a flat*	
Mortgage	——————	Rent	——————
Water Rates	——————	Water Rates	——————
Service Charge	——————		
Ground Rent	——————		
Insurance	——————		
Repairs	——————		
Total	======	Total	======

Renting a place may be cheaper in the short term, particularly if you need a large mortgage to help you to buy, but remember that, at the end, the place you buy will be yours. The place you rent will always be someone else's.

MORTGAGES

Few people of this generation, buy their first home outright. Most need the help of a bank, building society or mortgage company. Over the past decade, the amount that these institutions will lend to single people, or couples has increased dramatically. Gone are the days when you went cap-in-hand and were glad of any loan you could get. Now they welcome you, and given any encouragement will lend you plenty.

The time has come for you to impose a limit on yourself as to how much you can borrow. After all you are the one that has to make the monthly repayments. Falling behind on your mortgage is at first stressful, then overwhelming, because ultimately, if you continue to miss payments, your house will be sold to pay off the debt. So, keep the initial borrowings under control – your control. This is what I think you should use as your rule of thumb. You should borrow no more than three times the main income, plus one times the secondary. That means, if the husband earns £15 000 a year, and the wife £8000 you should borrow

$$3 \times £15\,000\ (£45\,000) + £8000 = £53\,000$$

or net monthly payments (that is what you pay) should be less than a quarter of your total monthly salary. The couple on £23 000 a year should keep payments below £480 a month. At 13 per cent that would fund a mortgage of £52 000.

MIRAS

At some stage the word MIRAS will be mentioned. The letters stand for Mortgage Interest Relief At Source. It just means that tax of 25 per cent has been taken off the repayments for the first £30000 of your mortgage (or all the mortgage if it is less than £30000). And that is tax relief taken care of – you pay the repayments net. (You no longer get tax relief at the higher rate, so even if you pay tax at 40 per cent you will only qualify for tax relief at 25 per cent.)

WHICH MORTGAGE?

There are about 10 to 15 different mortgages on the market at the moment, but most are variations of two basic types: the repayment and the endowment. It is worth bearing in mind that anyone who sells you an endowment mortgage gets a commission of around £800 on a £50000 mortgage. There is no commission for selling a repayment mortgage. Although the rules say that salesmen have to offer what is known as 'best advice', the commission may colour the judgement of the less scrupulous. Take the time to work out for yourself which is the most suitable mortgage for your financial circumstances.

Repayment

This is the simplest type to understand. You borrow the money and you pay it back, with interest, over the number of years that you have agreed, usually 25 years. So every month you pay back a combination of interest and capital and, at the end of the term, the loan is paid off and the house is yours.

Endowment

With an endowment you take out a loan and an insurance policy. You borrow the money that you need and pay only the interest on it for the term (say 25 years). At the same time you take out an endowment policy into which you pay a monthly premium. Over 25 years (and the term of the endowment policy will always match that of the mortgage) the policy should grow to equal or beat the size of the mortgage. On Pay-off day the endowment policy is cashed in, the mortgage paid off and the balance comes to you. In the meantime, if the policyholder dies, the mortgage is paid off.

With a repayment mortgage you can take out a mortgage protection plan that will pay off the mortgage if the policyholder dies. If you are single, particularly a single man, watch out. Single people may not want to pay for a mortgage protection policy. After all, if they have no dependants and they die, the house or flat can be sold to pay off the mortgage without inconveniencing anyone. So why pay for the policy unnecessarily while you are alive. And single men are particularly heavily hit by premiums. The AIDS virus has made these types of policies very expensive for all single men.

Variations

Repayment There are two main types of repayment mortgage, which one you choose depends on your circumstances.

● The 'constant net repayment' mortgage is, in the long run, the cheaper of the two. It means that assuming interest rates remained the same for the life of the mortgage (which of course they won't) then you would pay exactly the same every month.

● With the 'gross profile' repayment mortgage the repayments are calculated differently. You pay less in the early years and more in the later years.

Endowment There are four main types of endowment mortgage for the ordinary borrower. Though every year there seem to be a growing number of variations on the variations. But if you understand the main four, you will have no difficulty picking up the new types.

● A 'with profits' endowment mortgage is the most expensive and not used much nowadays. The insurance premiums are pitched high enough to ensure beyond any shadow of a doubt that at the end of the 25-year term, your mortgage will be paid off and you will get a good sum to yourself. Ideal, but expensive.

● A 'guaranteed' or 'non-profit' endowment mortgage guarantees to pay off your mortgage at the end of the term, but gives you no extra. It is quite expensive and poor value. Avoid this if you can.

● A 'low cost' endowment is a popular choice for home buyers. It runs like its big brother the 'with profits' endowment, except that the monthly premiums are smaller, so the subsequent lump sum is smaller. At the end of the term it should be large enough to pay off the mortgage, though that is not guaranteed, and leave you a little extra. But the great benefit is the smaller premiums.

● If you want really small premiums in the early years you could opt for a 'low start, low cost' endowment. This runs like a low cost endowment, but the premiums are weighted in your favour in the first five years. You pay less in the first year and more in every subsequent year up to year five. Then you have to make up the difference over the rest of the life of the mortgage, so for the next 20 years you pay slightly more than you would otherwise have done. It may suit you if you are going to be stretched in the early years.

Another popular alternative to help in the early years is a new type of endowment, currently only available from some building societies. It works like this: you borrow an extra, say, £5000 and that money is used to reduce your repayments in the first three to five years. You then go onto the proper level for the remainder of the mortgage. The £5000 has gone and you have a larger mortgage to pay off, but at least you got through the early part of the mortgage when you would otherwise have been over-stretched.

This type of mortgage is very good if you know that at the end of the five years your income will be going up. Perhaps you will have a much better job because your training is finished, or your wife will be going back to work or working part time because the children will be at school or interest rates are likely to fall. Or whatever. But they are hopeless for people in the opposite position.

WATCH OUT Don't take on a low start mortgage if you are buying as a couple and intend starting a family in a few years. Your repayments will probably be going up just as some income is lost if the wife leaves work to have a baby.

Others
There are other types of mortgages – pension, unit linked, unit trust, PEP – which suit specific types of people. They are not run of the mill home loans and unless you are fairly financially sophisticated, I would give them a miss.

Fixed rate mortgage This is an option that may suit you if you are on a tight budget and can take no risk with interest rates going up. Not all banks and building societies offer it. It works like this: when you take out your mortgage the interest rate is fixed, usually for one to three years. No matter what happens to interest rates during that period your monthly repayments don't change. If rates go up, you are quids in, if they go down you will be left stranded at the higher rate, but at least you will know you can afford the payments. At the end of the period you can switch to a flexible rate mortgage (one that goes up and down with interest rates in general) or take out another fixed rate term if one is available.

WATCH OUT Don't go for a foreign currency mortgage. You might be lured into thinking they are a good idea if French, German or Japanese interest rates are much lower than ours. But you can get badly stung if the currency moves against the pound. This is a mortgage for the professionals.

Annual Review
Most new mortgages have what is known as an annual review. It means that the repayments are set for 12 months. At the end of that year, they are

recalculated to take account of any interest rate movements in the previous 12 months. It cushions you from an increase in rates but stops you getting immediate relief from a decrease. It is set up really to save the bank or building society the expense of notifying customers every time there is a rate change, but it does help borrowers to budget for a full year.

> *TIP* · Even if you are on an annual review you can ask to come off it, as you may want to do if interest rates are coming down sharply.

Other Expenses
Once you have got your mortgage set up and have started to buy your home you will begin to realise how much everything is going to cost you. But don't forget to take account of the other bills you will have to pay.

Stamp duty That is one per cent of the price of the property if it costs more than £30000. It is paid when you buy.

Survey Most people have a property surveyed before they buy. It should show up any defects which a professional surveyor will find, but your untutored eye might miss. A bank or building society must have a valuation before they lend money on the property. You should go further and have a house buyer's report or, if you can afford it, a full structural survey. It will cost between £150 and £350 on a £40000 house.

Solicitor It is difficult to buy a house without using a solicitor. You can do it yourself, but I wouldn't recommend it. With an investment of this size, you should pay a professional to check the legal side of things – either a solicitor or a licensed conveyancer. How much you are charged depends on the value of the property and the amount of work that is done. Ask about hourly rates in advance.

You will also have extras to pay: perhaps an arrangement fee to the bank or building society; removal costs; the gas, electricity and telephone meters will have to be read and if you are unlucky reconnected and, of course, the bottle of champagne when you finally move in. So make sure there is a bit in the kitty.

> *TIP* · As soon as you decide the size of your mortgage, start a Specific Savings Account. Deduct your current rent from the proposed monthly mortgage repayment, and save the rest. You will soon know if you can afford it – and that is a lesson worth learning – and it will give you something in the kitty for all the extra bills you will have to pay when you finally find the home of your dreams.

Buying a Council House
You can buy your council home, at a discount, if you have been a council tenant for more than two years. The longer you have been a tenant the more you will get off, as the table shows.

	Discount %	
Qualifying period	*Houses*	*Flats/maisonettes*
2 years	32	44
5	35	50
10	40	60
15	45	70
20	50	70
25	55	70
30	60	70
over 30	60	70

To keep the discount, you have to live in the house for three years after buying it. Otherwise you will have to pay back some of the discount.

To buy, you have to take a number of steps, in the right order and at the right time. First of all pick up form RTB 1 (right to buy 1) at your local town hall, fill it in and return it. You will then get, within a couple of months, form RTB 2 which confirms your right to buy. A Section 125 notice will be sent to you, giving you the price of the house or flat, less any discount that you are entitled to. At this stage you can appeal to the District Valuer if you think the price is too high. If he, or she, thinks it is too low then the price can be put up, so don't appeal unless you really do think you are being overcharged. Get a survey done, to make sure the property is sound. And set up a mortgage, if you need one. Then go ahead and complete as you would do with any other property.

You can drop out of the sale if you decide against the move, and you can put off buying for three years after a valuation, but still get the property at the same price. Or you could opt for shared ownership. But remember, when you cease to be a council tenant, and turn into a home owner you will become liable for repairs and the upkeep of your property. So allow money for that when you are working out the economics of buying.

Shared Ownership
This is a way of buying part of a house or flat, and paying rent on the rest. It allows you to get a foot on the housing ladder, even if you can't afford to

buy a place of your own outright. You have to be buying from a housing association, builder, new town or council (a private seller would be unlikely to offer this option). You can buy between 25 per cent and 90 per cent of the property initially, though you can go right up to 100 per cent by the end. If you buy 25 per cent, then you also pay 75 per cent of the rent, if you buy 50 per cent, then you will have to pay 50 per cent of the rent and so on. When it comes to selling, you can either sell your share on to someone else, or you sell the whole thing, while at the same time buying the rest of your share.

Further details of schemes, and a helpful booklet are available from The Housing Corporation, 149 Tottenham Court Road, London WC1P 0BN. Tel: 071 387 9466.

RUNNING INTO PROBLEMS

Around 45 000 people every year have their homes repossessed. That is the depressing final step that banks and building societies have to take if home owners find that they cannot, or occasionally will not, pay the mortgage. No one likes doing it. These are not numbers, they are families that are being made homeless, and the banks and building societies will do everything they can to stop it happening to you. But ultimately, if you allow huge arrears to build up, don't keep your lender abreast of your financial circumstances, and cannot pay your mortgage that last step is taken.

So don't let it happen to you. If you find your mortgage repayments are getting too much for you, there are several things you can do. First of all, work out if the problem is short term, medium term or long term.

Short Term

A short term problem is something where you can see, or almost see, an end to it. You might be ill and off work so you are not getting overtime, but you will soon be back and making the money again. Or you have been hit by an emergency, or you lost your job and it is taking you a few months to find a new one. You must go and see the building society or bank. Ask at the enquiries desk who you should speak to and explain what has happened. Don't worry, they won't be shocked, they have heard it all before and they will be able to help.

It is crucial that you speak to them before you start to build up arrears or you limit the options open to you. If you have a £500 a month mortgage and you don't pay for two months, you will have a £1000 debt to discuss too. You might find that the lender will be able to allow you to miss paying the mortgage for two or three months (that debt will then be added to your mortgage), or allow you to pay interest only for a few months until you are back on your financial feet. But remember they are not philanthropists. Any help you are given, you will have to pay for at the end of the mortgage.

Medium Term

This is the sort of problem that arises from, say, a sharp rise in interest rates or a change in your circumstances such as a wife becoming pregnant and having to give up work. You can't quite pay the mortgage at the level being asked, but you will be able to in the future.

There are options open to you here. The one that suits you will depend on which type of mortgage you have. Repayment mortgages are much more flexible than endowment. You might find that the first thing you have to do is switch from an endowment to a repayment.

WATCH OUT Agents who sell endowment policies get commission. Because of the way it is now paid they have to refund part of their commission to the company selling the policy if the policy is surrendered early. So that they don't lose out, some agents are inserting a '1% clause' into new policies. It means that the policyholder has to pay the agent one per cent of the value of the endowment policy if the endowment policy lapses. Check before you sign – and don't if it has a one per cent clause.

If interest rates have gone up, and you cannot afford the new level, you might be able to stay on the monthly payments you are making. That means when rates come down, you will have to continue on the rate you are paying until you have paid off the arrears you built up.

Or you could switch to a fixed rate mortgage. Again you might get caught out when interest rates come down, but at least it will have solved your current crisis.

Or you might be able to add a further, say, £5000 to your mortgage and use that to help fund the repayments for the next three to five years. You will only be able to do this if the value of the property is much larger than the mortgage.

You may also be able to increase the length of a repayment mortgage, perhaps up to 30 years to decrease the monthly payments. In extreme cases the lender may allow you to pay interest only for a while, but you would have to pay the capital back more quickly in future years to make up for this.

Long Term

There is only really one solution to a long term mortgage problem. Sell up. If you cannot afford the monthly repayments, and there is nothing in the immediate future which will change that, then you must get yourself a smaller mortgage. And that usually means selling your current property and buying a cheaper one. The sooner you make your move, the more money you could take out of the property. If you let the arrears build up then there could be nothing left for you. So put your home on the market at a realistic price and try to sell quickly.

If the value of the house or flat is lower than the mortgage, some people try putting the keys through the letterbox of the building society or bank and walking away from the problem. They can't. They are still responsible for the mortgage. The lender will sell the house, but you will still have to make up the difference between the size of the mortgage and price the house was sold for.

If you are unemployed the DSS may help with the mortgage payments. People on Unemployment Benefit get half the interest of the mortgage paid for the first 16 weeks they are unemployed, then all the interest will be paid, but none of the capital. It may be a temporary solution to your problems, but it won't be a permanent one.

The important thing about dealing with mortgage problems is to go and see your lender as soon as possible. Don't wait until your non-payment trips the computer and you get a strongly-worded letter. The earlier you go the more sympathetic will be the ear you get, but don't go empty handed. Expecting them to come up with a solution is not the answer. Think about the problem before you go.

Make an appointment, so you know that you are telling your problem to the right person and have some idea of a solution. Outline the reasons why you cannot pay the mortgage at the moment and explain why you think you will be able to pay in the future. Or detail your proposals for selling your home. With that sort of positive outlook, your lender should be as helpful as possible.

Arrears That Have Built Up

If you already have an arrears problem, and your mortgage is just one of many debts, then you need professional debt counselling. Go to a money advice centre, a CAB, or phone the National Debtline on 021 359 8501. And read Chapter 6.

12 · Becoming a Mum

Finding out that you are expecting a baby is a wonderful experience. Whether it was planned or accidental, once you have come to terms with the shock you will no doubt be excited, happy, thrilled, even a little nervous. It is unlikely that the financial implications will cross your mind. Let them. Having a baby is an expensive business. You don't realise how expensive until you start shopping for the new arrival: pram, cot, clothes, nappies, push chair, maternity wear, doing up a nursery of some sort, toys . . . The list is endless.

If the mum-to-be has been working up to now you will be losing part of your income just as the expenses increase. So take advantage of any cash that is on offer. Start with the DSS.

There are two main benefits for mums-to-be:
■ Statutory Maternity Pay
■ Maternity Allowance

Statutory Maternity Pay
This is a weekly payment made by your employer. How much you get depends on how long you have worked for that company. To qualify you have to satisfy two basic rules:
● you must have been working for the same employer for the six months up to the 26th week of your pregnancy
● you must be paying National Insurance contributions

How much you get There are two rates of SMP: a lower and a higher rate.

To qualify for the higher rate you must have worked full time for the same employer for at least two years, or part time for five years. For that you will get six weeks SMP paid at 90 per cent of your weekly wage and 12 weeks at the lower rate, currently £44.50 a week. If you don't qualify for the higher rate, then you will get SMP for up to 18 weeks at the lower rate of £44.50 a week.

Which 18 weeks? You get SMP for 18 weeks starting the day you give up work to take your maternity leave. But you have some flexibility as to which 18 weeks you go for. There is a 13-week core period when you must take time off work and be paid SMP. That is the six weeks before the baby is due, the week it is due and the following six weeks. You can suit yourself when you take the other five weeks. You can have them all before, all after or split around the core period. Write to your employer at least three weeks before you intend starting your maternity leave, giving him the dates, and enclosing your maternity certificate (Form MAT B1) which you will get from your doctor or midwife 14 weeks before your baby is due. Your SMP will be paid to you in the same way as your wages, on a weekly or monthly basis.

TIP · This is the minimum that your employer will pay. You might find that your contract of employment entitles you to a better deal. It is worth checking.

Maternity Allowance

Working mums-to-be who don't qualify for Statutory Maternity Pay, perhaps because they are self-employed or have recently changed jobs, may get Maternity Allowance instead. To qualify, you must have been paying National Insurance contributions for at least six months of the year up to the 26th week of your pregnancy. You claim the money from the DSS by filling in Form MA 1 and attaching your Form MAT B1 that proves you are expecting a baby. If your claim is successful, you will receive £40.60 for 18 weeks. As with SMP, you have some flexibility as to which 18 weeks you stop work for providing you make sure you stick with the 13 week core period.

If you can't get Statutory Maternity Pay or Maternity Allowance, and are on a low income, there are other avenues open to you. You may be able to get Income Support, Housing Benefit or, if you already have children, Family Credit. Ask the DSS for the appropriate forms. Or you could apply for a Maternity Payment from the Social Fund to buy necessities for the baby. To qualify for this, you, or your partner, must be on Income Support or Family Credit. This payment does not have to be repaid. You can also apply for a loan from the Social Fund but this money is not an outright payment. You will have to pay it back.

Other Help For Mums-to-be

All expectant women are entitled to free prescriptions and free dental treatment for the nine months of their pregnancy and for a year after the baby's birth.

To get your medicines free, fill in Form FB 8 (available from your doctor or midwife) as soon as you know you are pregnant.

To get your dental work free, tell the dentist before he starts a course of treatment. Only NHS work is free, any private dental treatment will still have to be paid for.

If you are on Income Support you will also get:
> free milk – up to seven pints a week
> free vitamins
> help with fares to and from the hospital for ante-natal visits
> And you may get a Social Fund loan to help with buying maternity
> clothes.

RETURNING TO WORK
By law, you are entitled to your job back after you have had the baby, providing you have worked full time for the same employer for two years or part time for five.

But you have to do the following:
- Three weeks before you take your maternity leave, write to your employer asking for your job to be kept open. Tell him when you intend returning. This letter holds your job, but doesn't commit you.
- Seven weeks after the birth your employer will write and ask if you still want your job back. Reply within three weeks giving him the date of your return.
- If he doesn't write to you, then you take the initiative within nine weeks of the birth.
- Be back at work within 29 weeks of the birth.

Child Benefit
Once you are a mum, you will get child benefit which is paid until your baby reaches the grand old age of 16 (or 19 if he or she stays in full time education). Fill in form FB 8 and attach the Birth Certificate and you will get £8.25 a week if it is your first child, or an additional £7.25 a week if you are already claiming for another child or children.

One Parent Benefit
If you are a single parent you will also get One Parent Benefit. This amounts to £5.60 a week, no matter how many children you have got.

Useful DSS Leaflets
NI 17A A Guide to Maternity Benefits
FB 8 Babies and Benefits (which has an application form for Maternity Allowance, Child Benefit, and One Parent Benefit)
FB 27 Bringing up Children?
CH 11 One Parent Benefit
AC 2 Now there is an easier way to get your Child Benefit.

TWINS, TRIPLETS . . .?

One baby is expensive, but having them two, or even three at a time, will push the costs sky high. If you are worried, you can insure against it, but be warned it is pricey. Providing you are not on fertility drugs, or have had a scan, just fill in a proposal form before the ninth week of your pregnancy.

What it costs depends on several factors
- how old you are (the older you are the more likely is the chance of twins)
- whether there is a history of twins in your family
- how much you want to insure for

A woman in her late thirties is at the peak of her time for conceiving twins, and if you have already got one set, then you are likely to have another. So a 39-year-old with twins would be charged £10 per cent – that means the premium would be 10 per cent of the lump sum you are insuring. If you want a £1000 lump sum in the event of having twins or triplets or more, it would cost £100.

A 21-year-old with no history of twins in the family would only be charged £2 per cent, that is £20 to insure a £1000 lump sum. The problem here is that the minimum charge is £50.

Once the baby is born, you will start looking to its financial future. Whether you want to invest the child benefit, make the best use of money given at the christening, and in later years, on birthdays and Christmases, or want to go all the way and save for school fees, move on to Chapter 13, 'Children and Money' – not that the two ever go together!

13 · Children and Money

Children and money seem to fit together better if one thinks about spending money, rather than saving it or investing it. Whatever joy they might bring into your life, children certainly take a lot of cash out of it.

They don't come completely empty-handed. All children bring two financial assets with them when they are born: a tax free allowance of their own, which means few children are tax payers; and a child benefit allowance.

Child Benefit

At present almost seven million families claim child benefit. You get £8.25 a week for the first child and £7.25 a week for every other child you have, and that figure should rise every year. You can claim – initially using form FB 8 – until a child is 16, or until a child is 19 if they continue in full time education. Mums usually get the money, but if you are separated, Dads can claim if the child lives with them. You don't have to be married to get child benefit.

Tax Free Allowance

Although child benefit goes to the parents, the tax free allowance belongs, very firmly, to the child. The Inland Revenue see a child as a single person up to the age of 18 and gives them a personal tax allowance, currently £3295. That means they can have an income, from whatever source, up to that amount in this tax year, and pay no tax on it. Since few children have an income of anything like that, it means in reality that most children and youngsters are non-tax payers. They should invest what money they do have accordingly. If a youngster marries below the age of 18, s/he will lose her/his 'child' status, and the Inland Revenue will treat them like any other married person.

Whose Money is it Anyway?

There is one other issue which affects the child's tax status and that is where the money has come from.

HM Inspector of Taxes does not like tax cheats. And he certainly does not like the idea of rich parents putting their money in the child's name to avoid paying tax on the interest. To close this loophole, the Inland Revenue allows parents to give children enough money in one tax year to produce an income of £100, but no more. If it exceeds that then the money is deemed to be the parents' and taxed at their rate of tax. Money which comes from rich grandparents, or wealthy friends, or any other source whatsoever, will not be liable for tax, providing that the annual personal tax allowance is not breached.

INVESTING FOR BABIES
Parents, godparents, and grandparents often want to invest for babies. You see the little bundle of joy kicking its tiny feet, but you look ahead to the strapping 18-year-old who will want everything life has to offer. You know that you have 18 years to turn even a modest amount of savings into a sizeable nest egg, and you realise that for once in your life you are in with a chance of doing it. Time and planning are on your side. So, where do you put the money.

Friendly Societies
Friendly Societies often run special schemes for adults wanting to invest money for babies. They are in fact unit linked endowment policies, but they often have names such as Baby Bonds. You make annual or monthly payments (up to a maximum of £150 a year or £13.50 a month) for at least 10 years and the money is usually invested in shares or gilts, so it is low risk.

Savings Accounts
If you don't want to take any risk at all, opt for a bank, building society or National Savings account. Remember that the child is not a tax payer, so go for an account that pays interest gross (without deducting tax from the interest) or fill in an exemption form at your local bank or building society branch.

Watch out for the 'joined-up handwriting' rule. Most banks, building societies and the National Savings will not allow withdrawals from a child account until the child is seven and can sign its own name in joined-up handwriting. Or they will ask why you want the money and if the reason does not benefit the child they won't give it to you. Even if it is for the child's benefit, most of us object to being asked at all. To avoid this, make sure a parent is the trustee of the account.

Shares
For once the investment decisions are fairly easy. You know that you don't want income from the money, you want capital gain so that the money grows over the 18 years. And you should be prepared to take a bit of a risk. By any standards 18 years is a long term investment, so that should minimise the chance of your investment falling in value. So I would link

into shares. Choose either a lump sum or a regular savings plan and go for a unit trust or an investment trust. Both offer schemes that allow you to put regular amounts in, or twice yearly sums if you just want to add cash at birthday and Christmas, or just invest lump sums when you have them. For further details write to the Unit Trust or Investment Trust associations (details in Chapter 9).

Once you understand how these trusts work, you will know that you can go for a safe, steadily growing fund, or something a bit riskier, such as an oil, or gold, or Far East fund.

If you are prepared to monitor the fund, keep an eye on whether it is going up or down, and switch the money around as you see fit, then you could try one of the riskier options. But if you just want to leave the money where it is, and collect the payout at some later date, use a general growth fund.

Children cannot hold unit or investment trusts in their own name until they are well into their teens, so you would have to hold them as guardian. Nonetheless the child can claim back the tax on any dividends that are paid out.

Investing for Youngsters

Once children reach the age of around seven, a sea change takes place in their world of money. For one thing, they want to start doing some saving for themselves, and for another, they will start to tap you for pocket money. It might only have been a tanner a week when you were a child, but things have changed since then. It can run into pounds.

According to Walls, who publish a Pocket Money Monitor every year, this is the average weekly pocket money that children get. And Scottish children do better than English.

Year	boys	girls	5–7	8–10	11–13	14–16
1987	219p	220p	84p	121p	228p	458p
1988	213p	201p	100p	154p	236p	351p
1989	273p	269p	124p	161p	280p	605p
1990	323p	385p	129p	190p	353p	916p
1991	411p	381p	148p	235p	401p	920p

Of course there are also the handouts from friends and relatives, though, according to the research, these are not as generous as the parents' contributions:

1991	96p	80p	71p	70p	105p	116p

At this age, it is a good time to start instilling savings habits into children. Up to around the age of 10, children like to save just to see their money mounting up. They will put their 50p a week, or whatever their pocket money is, into a piggy bank and just count it every so often, to see it grow. You will still be expected to buy everything they want or need. The idea of using some of their own money to buy a new toy, or for rides on the fairground, is not a natural reaction. You should start to make it one.

Too many youngsters in their late teens or early twenties have got themselves seriously into debt because they have never learnt the basic facts of financial life. Saving up and then buying something is a healthy money habit. Buying on the never, never is not. And the sooner they learn to save before spending, the less likely they are to take on too much credit when they are older.

Once the piggy bank begins to fill, encourage your child to open a savings account. They will get interest on the money – so it will be worth more – and they will get used to dealing with banks and building societies. These institutions are in our High Streets to sell us something – loans, savings accounts, mortgages, financial services. So a customer should be no more nervous of them, than of the local supermarket. The sooner you get your child used to them, the less nervous they will be of asking for loans, or opening savings accounts when they grow up.

Most banks and building societies have special accounts for children, usually offering some sort of cartoon character-linked free gift. Use one of these (whichever offers the best deal) when the child is ready to open one. And remember to sign an exemption form so that the interest is not taxed. Don't use this account if there is a large sum of money to be deposited. There are two reasons for this.

Firstly, those accounts don't always offer a very good rate of interest, and secondly, remember the account is the child's. That means that they operate the account and can go in and withdraw every penny if they like. The bank or building society is not allowed to ask your permission before paying up. Limit them by moving large sums to an account where you have to give notice, and that may stop them emptying it to buy a new BMX bike, or whatever. Alternatively, you could hide the pass book!

Longer Term
Those who started a long term investment plan for their children when they were babies, will see them grow well by the time they are aged seven. If you want to start at this stage, your choices will be much the same. Go for something linked to shares or gilts and you should see capital growth rather than just interest being added to your money. You have still got the

best part of a decade to go before your child comes of age, so you don't have to worry too much about the ups and downs of the stock market. In 10 years it should be much higher than it is now.

As the time approaches for you to take the money out, keep an eye on the financial pages of the paper. If the stock market is soaring away to record highs, then think about cashing in. Shares, like trees, do not grow to the sky, so get out before they fall back again. You may not get the very best price for your units or shares – no one gets out at the very top of a market – but at least you won't have let the profit go and still be holding on to your investment as it slips back down again.

Investing for School Fees

More than half a million parents in Britain have opted out of the state education system to send their offspring to private schools, at enormous expense. It is estimated that a child starting at an independent school this month will cost the parents over £100000 by the time he or she comes out 13 years later. Few parents can afford that sort of money so it is comforting to know that there is help available.

It is known as the Assisted Places Scheme and is backed by the Government. Some 6000 places are available every year at independent day schools, and some boarding schools will also help with the cost of living-in. It is a means-tested benefit and fees will be paid in full for the child if parents earn less than £8000 a year, after allowances have been deducted for other dependent children. Fees are then paid on a sliding scale up to a cut-off point when relevant parental income reaches £19000.

Further details are available from the Department of Education and Science, Room 3/65 Elizabeth House, York Road, London SE1 7PH; the Welsh Office Educational Department, Crown Offices, Cathays Park, Cardiff CF1 3NQ; the Scottish Education Department, Room 4/25 New St Andrew's House, St James Centre, Edinburgh EH1 3SY.

If you plan to pay the fees yourself you have three choices
- investing a lump sum
- making regular savings
- paying out of income

Investing a lump sum If you start with a capital sum, a scheme can be tailored for you by one of the large school fee specialists. The money for fees will be made available when you need it; at the start of the schooling or later in the child's education. The capital will be spread over several investments: building society accounts, index-linked National Savings certificates, unit and investment trusts and personal equity plans. It is reckoned that £100 000 invested now would put three children from age 11 through London day schools, or send two to boarding school. Most people have somewhat less to earmark for fees, but it is still possible to guarantee at least part of future cost using an educational trust. The money will be used to buy an annuity which guarantees the fees at a certain date. For example £5000 invested now with one plan guarantees around £400 a term for 15 terms starting a year after the investment.

Making regular savings A savings plan for school fees should be started as early as possible to allow it time to grow before you start to call on it to pay out. But they are pricey. Premiums of £800 a month, started four years before you need the money, would pay for three children to go to a day school or two to board. Most people try to save around £150 a month, and top up the fees out of income.

Paying out of income If you don't start a savings plan and haven't a lump sum you will have to pay out of income. That will be a struggle because there are no tax advantages. Your money is taxed before you pay the fees. Some parents try to pay the fees by taking out a loan on their home, but this should only be seen as a last resort, because you will still be paying off the loan, long after the children have moved on from school.

TEENAGERS
By the time children become teenagers, they will have split, financially, into two groups. Those who believe that money was made round to go round, or made flat to pile up. Upbringing doesn't always have a lot to do with it. Two children from the same family can have completely opposing views on what to do with their money: one will spend everything, the other will save up to buy what they want.

At this point do make every effort you can to guide a spendthrift back onto the rails. Every year hundreds of youngsters end up in Citizens' Advice Bureaux trying to find a magic formula to get them out of a morass of debt that they shouldn't have got into in the first place. There is no such magic. They can and often do spend the next ten years paying back what they owe. You can save your children from that fate by some judicious guidance now.

DO-IT-YOURSELF
Most teenagers will want to run their own bank or building society account. And most will know exactly which one they want to go to. The

major High Street savings institutions all offer free gifts to lure the youngsters into their branch. It could be free pairs of jeans, cameras, record tokens, membership of a club, even a cash bribe, so let your child choose which one suits best.

If they don't know what is on offer he or she can go in and get leaflets from all the local branches and then decide. You will find that the rates of interest may not be top class but they will be good enough for small amounts of savings. The youngsters should use these accounts to save. Putting in pocket money, earnings from paper rounds and Saturday jobs to save up for school trips, new bikes, clothes and videos instils a good habit.

Once they reach 14, youngsters can be offered plastic cards for withdrawing money from ATMs (hole in the wall machines). That gives them access to between £100 and £250 a day, depending on the bank or building society and whether they have that sort of cash in the account. There are no facilities for overdrawing. Don't be tempted into guaranteeing an overdraft for them. That would not do anyone any favours.

INVESTING FOR TEENAGERS

By the time children get into their mid teens, your investment priorities will be changing. If you have any money to invest for them, you won't want to tie it up for considerable periods. Chances are they will need the money in a few years time for a deposit on a flat, to help with further education courses, maybe to buy a first car or pay for a decent holiday. The problem is you don't know, so you shouldn't be linking into anything where it might be difficult to get the money out again. That includes investments such as shares or unit and investment trusts. Although you can easily get your money back the timing may not be right. You might need the cash just when depressing economic news has sent the stock market into a tail spin and your investment is at a low point. This is a time for using high interest savings accounts – maybe going for a 90 day account – where you have to give three months' notice on the money, or perhaps even a 12 month bond if you feel you could tie the money up for a year.

If the children are still in their early teens, try the National Savings Children's Bonus Bond. You can buy up to £1000 worth of bonds, in multiples of £25. Hold them for five years, and a good bonus will be added (see page 73). They work like savings certificates so if you cash them in early your return will be reduced.

LEAVING SCHOOL
Becoming a Student

School leavers that go on to further education will have a few more years of juggling their cash. Many who get a full grant find that it is the largest sum of money they have ever had in their hands at one time. Budgeting becomes crucial, so make sure the cash lasts as long as it is meant to. They should open a bank account at a branch near the campus. These branches are geared up to helping students, and often have a student counsellor wise in the ways of student problems, particularly on what to do if the grant doesn't come through when it is meant to.

The banks will also offer substantial perks to students opening an account with them and depositing their first grant cheque. It may be money in the account, free overdraft facilities, free banking or some sort of free gift or vouchers. They should choose the one that suits them best. By the time they get to their university or polytechnic, students should have their grants lined up. They are also able, now, to apply for an interest free loan to top up the grant. This has to be paid back once they start working, but it may help them to budget better in their student days. Full details are available at the students' union.

Summer Work
Students who don't get a job in the vacations are not able to claim Income Support, unless they are disabled or single parents. They are unlikely to qualify for Unemployment Benefit because it is based on National Insurance contributions, something most students will not yet have made.

If they take a job, they will be able to earn the first chunk of money tax free, up to the single person's allowance. But, like everyone else they only have one allowance. So if part of it is used up on tax free interest from savings accounts, they won't be able to earn so much, tax free, in the summer vacation. Grants do not come into the tax-free allowance.

Further Training
School-leavers who don't have a job to go to are guaranteed further training through the Government-backed training schemes. They will be paid a training allowance of at least £29.50 a week if they are 16, or £35 a week if they are older than that. While they are doing this training they should make sure they keep a record through the National Record of Achievement. It is a *This Is Your Life*-type book – a red hardback which will include everything of interest and value they do. No doubt school leavers would start by slotting in any educational qualifications they have. As they went through training, they could add any other achievements, qualifications, or activities and any jobs they had had. They would then take this with them when they applied for jobs.

If they are over 18 and have not had a job for at least six months, they can get a training place under the adult scheme. They will be paid a training allowance equal to their weekly benefit entitlement plus an extra £10. They can also apply for a Career Development loan of between £300 and £5000, but this is a loan not a grant and will have to be paid back when they eventually get a job.

Starting Up in Business for Yourself

Many people with a good idea for making money, or a skill they want to develop decide to start up in business for themselves.

They are prepared to work hard for long hours to make a go of their business, but what brings them down is
- lack of cash at the beginning
- lack of business know-how

Well there is an answer to both these problems:

Cash The Enterprise Allowance is run by the local TECs (Training and Enterprise Councils) under guidelines laid down by the Government. If they think your business plan is viable and that you will be able to make a go of your business they can pay you between £20 and £90 a week for between 26 and 66 weeks to help you in the early days. How much you get depends on your needs and the needs of other people in your area.

Business help There are plenty of people and courses around now to help you put your business on a sound managerial footing. Your local college or polytechnic might run open courses to allow you to train in computers or business skills; you could attend day-long enterprise awareness events; or ask at your local Jobcentre or TEC about local services. Try also Instant Muscle, a charity set up to help unemployed young people start their own businesses (84 North End Road, London W14 9EF. Tel: 071 603 2504), or Livewire which offers free business planning advice and action packs (60 Grainger Street, Newcastle Upon Tyne. Tel: 091 261 5584).

Moving Out

Moving away from home, into a flat, bedsit or lodging is a more major move than you might think. There is all the fun of being on your own and in control of your own life and your own finances. But watch out, you will lose your safety net too. By safety net, I mean parents. As often as not when you were stuck before they would step into the breach with a loan, or an outright gift. That won't be available once you start running your own finances. Suddenly you find that you have a mortgage or rent to pay, community charge, fuel bills, food to buy, fun to pay for, some furniture to get, a holiday, the car breaks down, the washing machine floods . . . and there is no money in the kitty to cover it all.

Stress points like that can hit a relationship hard. Whether you are living with a partner, or sharing with a group of friends, if you run out of money the arguments will start. Avoid this by getting into 'priority bill paying' fast. You have to have food, fuel, some fun and you have to pay the rent or mortgage and community charge. Or you will be homeless. But don't overspend on things like furniture just because you happen to have a bit of spare cash at the time. Always try to have some savings in a building society or bank account to give you a safety net of your own. If you put the money in an account that insists you give notice, even as little as seven days, it will stop you being tempted to impulse buy.

'Keep out of debt' must be your motto.

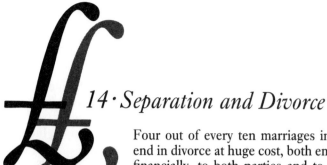

14 · Separation and Divorce

Four out of every ten marriages in this country end in divorce at huge cost, both emotionally and financially, to both parties and to any children. There are no winners in ordinary divorce cases.

For every million-pound financial settlement that the Ivana Trumps and Sarah Brightmans get from their husbands, there are thousands of wives who find that divorce pushes them very close to the poverty line.

Husbands fare little better. Separation and divorce will seriously damage your wealth as the same income has to stretch to finance two households. If times were tight before, they will be impossible now.

Gone are the days when courts insisted that a wife must be kept in the manner to which she has become accustomed; but in most divorces there is still a lot of unsightly haggling over the settlement, and in the end neither husband or wife is ever satisfied with the outcome.

First Steps

As soon as a couple separate – no matter who leaves whom – there are certain financial steps that should be taken particularly if an atmosphere of bitterness and hostility has already built up.

- Put a stop on all joint accounts. Let the bank or building society know that you are separated, and insist that all cheques or withdrawals from the account should have the signature of both parties. This stops one partner from clearing out the account or, worse still, from running up a huge overdraft for which the other will be liable.
- Stop any joint credit or store card agreements you have. Again your ex-spouse could run up a huge bill, and you would be liable. If you feel that this action would be seen as a hostile gesture at a time when the atmosphere is very tense anyway, use your own judgement as to how far you can trust your ex. Better a hostile atmosphere than a huge bill.
- If the family home is in the name of one partner the other must register their right to stay in the property at the Land Registry. This will also stop the home from being used as collateral for a loan.
- Tell the mortgage lender that you have separated. This is particularly important if the husband, who pays the mortgage, has moved out. The bank or building society must alert you as soon as one mortgage payment is missed otherwise you could have two or three months' arrears built up before you even knew that no one was paying. If you know that the

mortgage is still being paid, and is likely to continue to be, then don't tell the lender yet. It might precipitate action being taken that wouldn't be in anybody's interest. Just keep a check that the mortgage is being paid.

● Tell the DSS you have split up. You may be entitled to Income Support, Family Credit or Housing Benefit.

● Try to get a half hour fixed-fee interview with a solicitor specialising in family law. Go prepared with a list of questions and any necessary documents to make the most of the time, and by the end you should know what your next steps should be.

● Inform the Inland Revenue so that you will get any increased tax allowances that are your due, such as the Additional Personal Allowance if you have children.

● Tell the local authority so that you are not liable for your spouse's community charge.

Cost of Divorce

Financially, a divorce can be very expensive indeed. It is reckoned that a typical uncontested divorce can cost from £500 to £1000, in legal fees. If there is any sort of in-fighting over who gets what, then that bill can rise to many thousands more.

You can do it yourself. This is only really possible if the split is very amicable indeed, and there are no children involved. The petition costs £40, and you can get a form from your local county court, or the Divorce Registry, Somerset House, Strand, London WC2. You will need to pay about another £4.50 to sign an affidavit confirming that the details are true, and a further £10 when the decree absolute comes through.

Legal Aid

If you qualify for Legal Aid you may be able to get financial help with the legal fees connected with the costs of your divorce. However, this is not as easy and simple as it might seem at first sight. Legal Aid is not designed to let you dump all your legal bills on the state. It can be complicated and it is means tested. So if you have a good income or a reasonable amount of savings you won't qualify.

Even if you do fall within the scheme, the money that is paid to foot your legal bills will only be a loan. If you get a good settlement from your ex-spouse, then you may have to pay back the costs of the Legal Aid. If you get the house instead of a cash sum, then you may still have to pay back the Legal Aid, plus interest, in the years to come when you eventually sell up. So think hard before you climb aboard this particular wagon.

An alternative offered by some solicitors is to run up a bill, instead of charging as they go along. For instance, a wife may have nothing when she comes for legal help with her divorce. But she may have good prospects in the divorce when she gets her share of the home and assets. The solicitor may agree to work for her and wait for payment until after the divorce and, perhaps, even after the house is sold. This may be a better deal for some wives, than opting for Legal Aid. In fact, you may not have a choice. Many solicitors are loath to take on Legal Aid work because it is so badly paid.

Choosing a Lawyer

Very few people have a solicitor on tap. The only one they are likely to have had any dealings with before is the solicitor who bought or sold a house for them. That solicitor will almost certainly be the wrong person to handle your divorce, unless they also specialise in family law. He or she, however, may be able to hand you on to someone else in the office, or recommend someone. It is crucial to find a specialist in divorce who knows exactly what to do so as not to waste time (and your money) checking out facts and case histories. Ideally your solicitor should be a member of the Solicitors Family Law Association, and your local CAB will give you a list of the ones in your area.

Check out costs before you start. Lawyers now have to tell you what their hourly charge is. So ring up and ask. Divorce lawyers will charge anything between about £50 and £200, an hour, but typically you could expect to pay £50 to £100. They work out their fees on quite a simple principle. They charge you for the time they work on your case at their hourly rate, and they charge for telephone calls and letters. To keep the cost of your divorce down, try not to bother them continually. Imagine a taxi meter running in their office, clocking up every time you ring in, call in or write in with a query. That is not to say that you shouldn't get your questions answered, but there are three ways of keeping costs to a minimum.

● save up your questions and ask them all at one time

● try asking the solicitor's assistant. He or she will often know as much on basic points and will charge a lot less.

● don't use your lawyer for emotional support. If you feel you must talk to someone, make it a friend or relative who isn't charging £80 an hour.

In Scotland

The legal system in Scotland is different from that in England and Wales, so the legal side of divorce, too, varies from that south of the border.

If there are no children in the marriage and the couple can agree financially, then they can do the divorce themselves. Get a form from your local Sheriff Court, pay your £40 and that is it.

However, it can be helpful to take some legal advice, and that can be good value for money. A good half-way house can be to do your own divorce, but get some help beforehand from a solicitor. That way you cut the costs without getting into a legal muddle.

If there are children, or the couple cannot agree on the financial settlement, then you will have to use a lawyer. Under Scottish family law, the court will try to adhere to the Clean Break Principle, in dealing with each spouse's claim against the other. That means they would rather give a capital sum to the 'have not' partner, than a continuing maintenance payment. For example, they would prefer the 'have' to pay the 'have not' £10000 in one lump sum, than £1000 a year for 10 years.

Maintenance payments for children will always be a continuing obligation on both parents and would not be dealt with under a clean break payment.

Pension rights will also be written into the equation in Scotland. Difficult though they are to value, a pension and any life insurance policies that could pay out large lump sums in the future, will be considered by the courts before making the award so the other partner should not miss out on these valuable assets.

Divorce and Tax

Splitting up, tax-wise, is relatively straightforward. There are three distinct areas where different rules apply:

- separation
- divorce
- maintenance payments

Separation While a couple are married they will be entitled to the following tax allowances: each will have a personal allowance and the husband will have the married couple's allowance. Once they have separated, each will continue to have a personal allowance and in the tax year that they separate (and only that year) the husband will continue to get the married couple's allowance. If, however, there are children then the wife can claim an Additional Personal Allowance. If the children live with the father he cannot claim the Additional Personal Allowance because he gets the Married Couple's Allowance.

The following tax year, each partner claims the allowances to which they are entitled, so they would both get a personal allowance and the parent looking after the child or children would get an Additional Personal Allowance. No one would qualify for the Married Couple's Allowance.

Divorce The tax position of a divorced couple is a continuation of separation. You each get the allowances you are entitled to. This would mean that both the ex-husband and ex-wife would get a personal allowance, and if either was looking after the children they would get the Additional Personal Allowance.

Maintenance payments The rules on maintenance payments changed in March 1988. Outlined below is the current system. I am assuming, throughout, that it is the husband who pays maintenance to the wife and children (and if it is the other way round substitute he for she, and she for he, in what is written below).

The husband will get tax relief on maintenance payments, up to the level of the Married Couple's Allowance every year. He pays the amount gross, that is without deducting tax, and his tax code will be changed to take account of the tax relief. To get this tax relief, the maintenance payments must be due under a court order or other binding agreement, not just a voluntary payment from the husband.

You won't get tax relief on:
- payments that are higher than the married couple's allowance (though you can still pay more)
- payments made to a child
- voluntary payments
- money that you already get tax relief on, that is, a mortgage

The wife does not pay tax on the money she gets – up to the married couple's allowance every year – nor does it count against her personal allowance. The system is set up to encourage an ex-wife to support herself. By continuing to have her personal allowance she can take a small part time job and still not be a tax payer.

TIP · If your maintenance order was set by the courts before March 1988, but you would prefer to be taxed under the new rules, ask your tax office for Form 142. But once you have switched, you can't go back.

Getting back together If you are reconciled while separated, tell the tax office. Your allowances will be switched back to their previous level, and the tax relief on maintenance payments (which you are no longer paying) will be stopped.

Remarrying If the husband gets married again, he will continue to get tax relief on his maintenance payments. If his ex-wife remarries, the ex-husband will lose his tax relief on the maintenance payments, and of course he won't have to pay anything for her upkeep any more.

Further details on tax and divorce are in a helpful little Inland Revenue leaflet IR 93 – Income Tax, Separation, Divorce and Maintenance Payments.

Mortgage Once you separate or divorce, the Inland Revenue sees you as two people again, so you will qualify for two chunks of mortgage tax relief. Not on the same property, though. You can each have tax relief of up to £30 000 on a mortgage.

Divorce and Pension
Once you divorce, a wife will lose her right to a widow's benefits and the husband's death in service benefit, since she will not be a widow on the husband's death. By the time a man gets into late middle age his pension rights can be very sizeable. Indeed in many cases they are worth more than the house, so this is a lot for the wife to lose. She and her lawyer should try to ensure that account is taken of this in the divorce settlement, particularly if the wife has spent much of her adult life at home bringing up the family and has not built up pension rights of her own. A separate insurance policy can be taken out to compensate her for this.

TIP · If maintenance payments make up most of a wife's income, she should insure them. After all if her ex-husband dies they will stop and she will be left with nothing. Term insurance is the best and cheapest answer. Take out a policy on the husband's life (you don't need his permission or signature), and it will pay up on his death within a certain time period. If, however, the man is over 40, these policies are very expensive, so try to get him to pay!

Divorce and Your Will
Divorce does not automatically revoke a will, so if you made one when you married – and you should have – it will still stand long after the marriage has failed. This could cause huge problems in the future if you have moved on to a new partner and had a new family.

Use a solicitor to write a new will for you. This is not a time to try and do it yourself. But don't think you can cut your ex-wife out altogether. If she and her children are financially dependent on you, they will have a claim on your estate.

Cutting the Cost of Divorce
The financial costs of divorce mount as a direct result of using your solicitor too much. The more the lawyers haggle over the assets and the longer it takes to sort out a financial settlement, the higher will be the legal fees at the end. So the easiest way to cut the cost of a divorce, is to cut the chat.

Round table discussion Go for a four-handed meeting to thrash out the problems. You and your solicitor should meet up with your ex and his/her solicitor and try to come to an agreement. When both lawyers are present tempers tend to be cooler and these meetings often churn out the basis of an agreement, but go into it with a spirit of compromise and a real will to agree.

Family Mediators' Association This is a more formal level of mediation and is only available in some areas of the country. It involves two professionals, usually a lawyer and a professional social worker, who help couples to solve the financial, emotional and child-related problems of their separation and divorce. It costs around £120 an hour and the FMA reckons most couples need three to six sessions. More details from the FMA, The Old House, Rectory Gardens, Henbury, Bristol, BS10 7AQ. Tel: 0272 500140.

Finally
Organising your finances while going through a divorce is never easy. The emotional strains of splitting up with what you thought was a lifelong partner make it particularly difficult for you to take a clear view of your money. You need to be able to stand back from the stresses of the divorce in order to sort yourself out.

The only way you can really do this is to have a checklist. Cover all these points to the best of your financial ability and you will then have the basis of a money agreement. It may not be as good as you'd want, but it's probably the best you'll get.

Divorce checklist
- If you and your spouse own a home, is the division fair to both of you?
- Is someone paying the mortgage at the moment?
- Who pays the mortgage after the divorce?
- Have you checked with the Inland Revenue to ensure you are getting all the tax relief you are entitled to?
- Tell the Inland Revenue if you are getting too much tax relief – they'll only claim the excess back later if you are
- If both parties are buying homes after the divorce, or separation, they'll both be entitled to tax relief up to £30,000

- Are you claiming all the DSS benefits you are entitled to?
- Make sure that your maintenance payments don't lift you marginally out of the benefits net – you might find the DSS payments are more regular
- Ensure that a wife doesn't let her entitlement to her husband's pension lapse – it could be worth a lot to her in later years
- Have you remembered to rewrite your will?

15 · Becoming a Widow

Dealing with death is never easy. Coping with the loss of your life long partner is doubly difficult because you will be faced with money problems and worries you have not coped with before. Even if you have been left fairly well-off, you might have to start dealing with financial decisions for the first time. Years ago, many women had to wait until their husband died to find out anything about his financial affairs. This is less frequently the case now, but a widow still has to deal with a batch of new money worries at a time when emotionally she feels raw and vulnerable.

The golden rule here is – don't rush. Many is the widow who has rued the day she paid off the mortgage, moved house, or invested in a flat in Spain, in the first few months after she was bereaved. This sort of financial decision can easily wait a bit longer and will be dealt with more easily at a later date. Of course there are some things you have to do immediately, like arranging the funeral and registering the death, but take your time over your other financial moves.

THE FUNERAL

If you have never arranged a funeral before, get help from the funeral director, your minister, or a relative. Don't expect it to come cheap. Nowadays the average cost of a funeral or cremation easily tops £1000. But there is help available from the DSS for those who can't pay.

If you, the widow, are on Income Support, Housing Benefit or Community Charge Benefit, you can apply for a Funeral Payment from the Social Fund. (You may not have been on Income Support prior to the death of your husband, but without his wage coming in, you might now qualify.) The payment will cover basic costs such as the funeral director, a coffin, one car, perhaps some flowers and the cremation or burial plot. Nothing more. If you want anything more elaborate, then you will have to pay for it yourself. Should your husband leave any money in his estate, then you will have to use it to repay the funeral costs to the DSS. But if there is no cash available, then the DSS will pay towards the cost of the funeral.

It is best to apply for the payment before the funeral (use form SF 200) and stick within the limits set. If you apply after, then you will need to produce the bill, rather than an estimate.

WIDOW'S BENEFITS

When your husband dies you change from being a wife to a widow. There is financial help that is yours by right. Widow's benefits, paid by the DSS, divide into three main categories:

- Widow's Payment
- Widowed Mother's Allowance
- Widow's Pension.

Claim the ones you are entitled to.

Widow's Payment

This is a lump sum of £1000. It is not means-tested so anyone can apply for it, regardless of how well off they are. You qualify if you are under 60 and your husband was still working when he died. It is dependent on his National Insurance contributions, not yours, and providing they were up to date, the money will be paid. You won't get the payment if you were divorced when your husband died, or separated, or living as a common law wife. It is a tax-free non-repayable sum.

Widowed Mother's Allowance

As the name implies this is a payment for widows with children. It is a weekly payment and is made up in two parts: a payment for yourself and a payment for the children. At the moment you get £52 for yourself, £10.27 for the first child and £9.70 for each of the others. This continues for as long as you are receiving Child Benefit. The money is taxable, but again, you won't qualify if you are divorced or living with another man.

Widow's Pension

If you are over 45 when your husband dies, or when your widowed mother's allowance ends, you qualify for Widow's Pension. But you can't claim the Widowed Mother's Allowance and the Widow's Pension at the same time. Again it is a weekly payment: £52 if you are between 45 and 54, slightly more if you are over 54. It is a taxable benefit and is paid until you reach the age of 60 and qualify for the state retirement pension. It will stop before that date if you move in with another man or remarry.

TIP · You may be entitled to more money every week. If your husband was a member of what is known as a contracted-out occupational pension scheme, or a personal pension scheme you are due an extra SERPS payment. Ask the company he worked for or the DSS to check this out for you.

Making a Claim
It is quite simple to claim any of these benefits. When you register your husband's death you will get a death certificate. Fill in the form on the back of this and you will be sent Form BW 1. That is the one you claim on.

━━━━━━━━ *Which benefit is for you?* ━━━━━━━━

Age when widowed	*What to claim*
Under 45; no dependent children	Widow's Payment
45–60; no dependent children	Widow's Payment Widow's Pension
Under 45; with or expecting a child	Widow's Payment Widowed Mother's Allowance
45–60 with dependent children	Widow's Payment Widowed Mother's Allowance
Over 60 but under 65	Widow's Payment Widow's Pension or Retirement Pension
Over 65	Retirement Pension

Useful leaflets from the DSS:
D 49 – What to do after a death
NI 51 – National Insurance for Widows
NP 45 – A Guide to Widows' Benefits
FB 29 – Help when Someone Dies

Other DSS Benefits
If you find you can't manage financially after your husband's death, try asking the DSS for help. There are other options open to them. You might qualify for Family Credit if you work over 24 hours a week, or Income Support and Housing Benefit if you don't work, or do under 24 hours a week. And if you are on Income Support you might get a grant from the Social Fund for specific expenses. But if you don't ask, you won't get anything.

TAX

Tell the Inland Revenue when your husband dies, in case you are due any tax rebate. You will get your personal allowance raised. A personal allowance is the amount of income you can have in one year before you are liable to tax. For a single person it is currently £3295 a year. In addition to this, widows get a Bereavement Allowance for the year their husband dies, and the following tax year. That allowance is currently £1720. If your husband died early in the tax year there may still be part of the Married Couple's Allowance unused that can be transferred to you. Your tax office will work out the figures for you.

If you are over 64 the personal allowances are slightly larger.
Age 65 to 74 – £4020
Age 75 and over – £4180.
The Bereavement Allowance does not change with age. There is no such thing as Widower's Bereavement Allowance – equality does not stretch that far.

If the widow, or widower, has children under the age of 18 then a further tax free allowance is paid. It is known as the Additional Personal Allowance and is currently £1720, regardless of how many children there are. There is a useful leaflet available from the Inland Revenue: IR 91 – Independent Taxation – A Guide for Widows and Widowers.

DEBT

You can't take it with you – your cash, that is – into the next world, but neither can you leave your debts behind. If you die penniless your debts will be written off. Credit cards, HP agreements, electricity, gas, phone . . . they will all close the accounts. If, however, there is money in the estate – a savings account, the house, insurance policies, pension payments – then that will have to be used to settle the bills. Check carefully to see if any loans had insurance policies attached which will pay up on death.

THE HOME
Renting

If your husband rented your home, either from a private landlord or the council, don't fear eviction. When he dies, write and tell the landlord and ask for the home to be put into your name. Providing you can pay the rent, all will be well. You can't be forced out unless you break the terms of your tenancy agreement, or stop paying the rent, and even then the landlord must go to court to get an order to repossess the house. If you cannot afford the rent because you are on a low income, you may be able to claim Housing Benefit, check with the DSS.

Mortgage

Visit the bank or building society and change the mortgage into your name. If your husband had a mortgage protection plan, or there was an endowment policy, you should find that the mortgage will now be paid off in full. That is what you have been paying the premiums for all these years. The bank or building society will give you the details. If you didn't have a policy then you will have to make the payments yourself. Widows with means can go ahead, but if you are not going to be able to fund the monthly repayments then you must do something now. If you work part time or are unemployed the DSS may be able to help.

This is not a time to sit on your hands and hope the problem will go away. The longer you put off doing anything, the larger the arrears become. The first step is to go and see the lender, that is the bank or building society that the mortgage is with. If you can't face the idea of talking about your financial problems to a stranger with power at a time when you are under enormous emotional stress, go to a CAB first. They will listen and help and probably come to the meeting with you.

The building society or bank may allow you three months' grace to get over the death of your husband. But the interest on the loan will still be clocking up, so this is a problem that may be better faced earlier rather than later. Work out if the problem is short or long term. Going out to work may allow you to fund the mortgage in future, so a sympathetic lender could allow you time to find a job, but ultimately the bill has to be paid. The longer you put off making payments, the larger the loan becomes.

If you are never going to be able to afford the mortgage, then you will have to consider selling up and moving somewhere smaller. Move as quickly as you can so that you will have some capital left for yourself when you do move. If you leave it too long the arrears will build up and you could be left with nothing, or worse still a debt when you do sell.

WRITING A WILL

Everyone should have a will. Lawyers make a lot more money sorting out the estates of people who die without one, than they ever do from writing the will in the first place. If you don't have a will you will die intestate, that is without a will. It means that your estate (all the money and assets you leave) will be divided up according to the law (and Scotland is different from England and Wales), and it can cause severe distress and in some cases hardship. For example, if a husband dies without leaving a will, only part of his money will go to his wife, the rest will go to the children. And that could mean that she has to sell the family home to give them their share – not something a distressed widow would want to cope with.

Do You Need a Lawyer?

No, you don't need a lawyer to draw up a will. You can do it yourself with ease. Just get a clean sheet of paper, write down your instructions, sign and date it in the presence of two witnesses (who are not beneficiaries); and that is it. Your will is made. Sadly, the pitfalls into which you can fall are endless. I don't think this is an option you should take. You could instead use one of the specialist will-writing companies such as Telegraph Willmaker, TrustDeed or Quill, or buy the *Which* pack for writing your will 'Make Your Will'. But these options still require quite a lot of work on your part.

The best solution for most people is to use a solicitor. It is the most expensive option in the short term, but it could prove to be the cheapest in the long run if it means that eventually your estate will be wound up quickly and simply. To keep costs low, make sure you know exactly what you want before you go into the lawyer's office. Don't sit there trying to decide whether you should leave your grandfather clock to your niece or nephew, and whether or not to give £100 to the bowling club. Go in with it all crystal clear in your mind, or better still on a piece of paper, and you shouldn't have to pay too much. Indeed, if you get a straightforward will written at a time when you are using a lawyer for a lot of other work, such as conveyancing your house, he or she may do the will for nothing.

> *TIP* · Important as it is for everyone to have a will, it is crucially important if you are living with someone to whom you are not married. In England and Wales, there is no such concept as a common law husband or wife. So they will get nothing when you die. Even in Scotland, where the concept is more accepted, they won't do well unless they can prove they were financially dependent.

Finally once you have written your will remember to leave it where it can be easily found, and make sure your nearest and dearest knows where it is. You may want to store it with the lawyer or with a bank, but a fire-proof box at home can be just as good an idea. It will work out a lot cheaper.

16 · Redundancy and Unemployment

Redundancy has been the making of some people. They have opted for voluntary redundancy, walked out of a good job on a Friday, banked a big fat cheque and started work somewhere else the following Monday. For most others, redundancy is a nightmare which puts huge emotional and financial strains on the family. You may work in an industry, hit by recession, where mass redundancy is expected, or it may come as a bolt from the blue. Either way you will be left, in days or weeks, with no job to go to, and perhaps more importantly no weekly or monthly salary.

You will have to start trying to find work again which can be difficult if unemployment is high in the area you live in, or your skill has been overtaken by technology, or you are just too old for most employers.

At least Fate does give you one card up your sleeve – a redundancy payment. If you are over 20 and have worked for your employer for more than 2 years you are entitled to a pay-off.

REDUNDANCY
What is Redundancy?
Redundancy is selling your job. In economic downturns workers are often paid off because they are surplus to requirements, or your firm may have decided to relocate to a different part of the country, or new equipment might have been installed that will take over your work, or the company might have gone into liquidation. For whatever reason your job is no longer there.

If it is just you that isn't needed, the job stays with someone else doing it, then that is plain old-fashioned firing. You won't get a redundancy payment, but if you feel you have been unfairly dismissed, you should seek advice about going to an industrial tribunal. Ask your union, or your local CAB, to help you with this.

Redundancy Payments
What you get when you are made redundant depends on
- your age
- how long you've been with the company
- your salary

The older you are, the longer you have been with the company and the more you earn, the higher will be the payoff.

Age and length of service – You are entitled to:

20–21 year olds	half a week's pay for each full year worked
22–41 year olds	one week's pay for each full year worked
41–60/65 year olds	one-and-a-half weeks' pay for each full year worked

There is a maximum you can claim of 30 weeks' worth of money, no matter how long you have worked for the firm and an earnings limit of £198 per week (and this rises every year). If you earn more than that, the surplus will be disregarded. This is the minimum that must be paid to you by law. Many firms are more generous with redundancy payments, particularly if they want to pay people off and are looking for voluntary redundancies.

If you are being made redundant because the firm has gone into liquidation, then it is unlikely there will be any money in the kitty for redundancy payments. Ask the liquidator for a leaflet called 'Employee's Rights on Insolvency of Employer' which will explain to you how to apply to the Government's redundancy fund for your money.

Redundancy Payments and Tax

Redundancy payments are tax free provided they are not written into your contract of employment. If they are, then anything over the statutory minimum will be liable for tax. Redundancy payments that are not part of your contract of employment – and most are not to get round this tax – will be free of tax up to £30000. Then you start to pay tax on the money at either 25 per cent or 40 per cent.

Golden handshakes amounting to more than £30000 are taxable, at your marginal rate. Anything under £30000 is tax free. Any other money you get when you leave, such as pay in lieu of holidays, will also be liable for tax in the normal way.

If the interest on your lump sum (and any other savings you have), together with your Unemployment Benefit, comes to more than your tax free allowance, you will have to pay tax on the excess at 25 per cent. But, remember, if you are married and your spouse doesn't work, you can move the savings into his/her name and have the use of their personal tax allowance too. (See page 83 for full details.)

What to Do With the Money

For many people a redundancy cheque of perhaps several thousand pounds will be the first large lump sum they have ever had. The temptation to install a new kitchen, buy a new car, or go on a decent holiday will be enormous. Don't be persuaded. That money is meant to tide you through the bad times, until you find another job. In times of high or rising unemployment that could be longer than you think, so use the money sparingly to run the household and pay the bills.

The best place for the cash is a high interest savings account. Put a small part of it into an easy access account, then you can probably afford to lock the rest of it up in a one or even three months' notice account. By putting it into a savings account you are not taking any risk with the money at all. It will always be there, with interest, for you to use.

If you are part of a large organisation that is making hundreds or even thousands of workers redundant, you might find that financial advisers will be laid on by the company, or might just get in touch with you off their own bat. Be wary about their advice. Don't be pushed into investing in something, such as endowment or assurance policies, or even unit trusts, unless that is what you want and what you feel is right for your circumstances. The salesman might be tempted to encourage you to opt for something that pays high commission to him, rather than something which is right for you. While your future is uncertain, you would do better to keep your money in an accessible, no risk account, rather than risk losing any of it, reaching for a better return.

WATCH OUT Don't be greedy. A promise of a better return than you think is possible usually involves, at best, a greater risk. At worst, the seller will run off with your cash.

UNEMPLOYMENT
Unemployment, in most cases, is the natural successor to redundancy. On the first day that you are out of work you should go down to your local Unemployment Benefit office and sign on. If you have paid enough National Insurance payments, and are actively looking for another job, you will get Unemployment Benefit, currently £41.40 a week. It doesn't matter how much you have in savings, this is not a means-tested benefit. If you are married you might be able to claim something for your wife or husband (or dependent adult as the DSS term them). Providing they earn less than the benefit you will get £25.55 a week. If you are over 55 and get more than £35 a week from an occupational or personal pension, then your Unemployment Benefit will be reduced.

If you still can't manage then you might be able to claim other benefits.
Family Credit If your partner is working over 24 hours a week, but on a low income.
Income Support People on a low income can apply for income support, but it will be reduced if you have savings. You will lose £1 a week for every

£250 (or part) of savings you have over £3000, up to a ceiling of £8000, when you won't get anything.

Housing Benefit and Community Charge Benefit These have a similar taper on the benefit as Income Support, but up to a ceiling of £16000.

If you fail to qualify for any of these benefits because your savings are slightly too high and you breach the £8000 level (or £16000), you might feel it is a good time to spend a little of your redundancy payment to bring it below the means-tested level. Don't blow it on a three piece suite and a colour TV, use it for something useful that will help you to manage while you don't have work. Or you could pay off a small part of your mortgage, say, to bring you down below the £8000 (£16000) barrier. Check also to see if you have any mortgage cover that will pay up if you lose your job.

Unemployment Benefit is paid for a year, thereafter you will get Income Support, if you qualify. But if you have savings of over £8000 you won't. This is all a bit of a minefield, don't get tripped up. Ask for help at a CAB because they know their way around, they have helped so many people like yourself.

TIP · Don't delay in going down to the UBO. Unemployment benefit cannot be backdated and if you don't claim, you won't get it.

Unemployment and Your Mortgage

The biggest worry for houseowners that have been made redundant is how to pay the mortgage. Check out your insurance policy in case there is a clause that covers your mortgage in the event of redundancy or unemployment. It is a hefty payment to meet every month when you are in work, it could be impossible once you lose your job. However, the DSS can offer some help here. For the first 16 weeks that you are out of work they will pay half the interest on the mortgage, thereafter they will pay all the interest. Most banks and building societies will accept these terms and add the arrears (that is the other half of the interest for the first 16 weeks) on to the amount you already owe. But the DSS will not pay capital payments or endowment premiums for you. If you cannot afford these yourself, you may have to reassess your financial situation. Those who think they will work again should go and see the lender, explain the circumstances and ask if the payments can be reduced or changed to interest only for a while.

Endowment premiums will have to be made otherwise the policy lapses. Those who will have difficulty getting another job, and can't afford the capital payments or endowment might have to sell up. For fuller details on what to do if you can't pay the mortgage, see pages 100–102.

GETTING ANOTHER JOB
Start by using any contacts you have made over the years, but if that fails to come up with anything move on to your local Jobcentre. Vacancies are displayed on cards, and if anything catches your eye ask for more details from the receptionist. She may be able to fix you up with an interview.

On your first visit to the Jobcentre or Unemployment Benefit Office ask to see a New Client Adviser who will help you to plan your job search and ensure that you are claiming all the benefits you are entitled to. If you have been out of work for more than four weeks, you may be able to get help with cost of fares to job interviews, ask at the Jobcentre before you go for any interviews.

Training
When you have been unemployed for over six months, and are between the ages of 18 and 59, you might be able to sign on for a retraining course. Financially, you will be better off because you will get a training allowance equal to your weekly benefit entitlement, plus £10 a week. You can also qualify for extra money for travel costs, rent, and if you are a single parent you might get child care costs. The longer you have been unemployed the more likely you are to get on a training course. Alternatively you could apply for a Career Development Loan. You can borrow between £300 and £5000 to help you pay for course fees, books, materials and so on. The loan is interest free while you are training, but once you get a job and start to pay it back, interest will be added.

Starting Up in Business for Yourself
If you can't get anyone else to employ you, you might think of starting up in business for yourself. This can be a tempting option, particularly if you have a hobby or skill that you think you could make money out of. You are probably prepared to work hard for long hours to make a go of your business, but the problems will begin if you have no money to start with and little business know-how. Well there is an answer to both those problems.

Cash   The Enterprise Allowance is run by the local TECs (Training and Enterprise Councils) under guidelines laid down by the Government. If they think your business plan is viable and that you will be able to make a go of your business they can pay you between £20 and £90 a week for between 26 and 66 weeks to help you in the early days. How much you get depends on your needs and the needs of other people in your area.

Business help   There are plenty of people and courses around now to help you put your business on a sound managerial footing. Your local college or polytechnic might run open courses to allow you to train in computers or business skills; you could attend day-long enterprise awareness events; or ask at your local Jobcentre or TEC about local services.

17 · Planning for Retirement

It is a pretty safe bet that anyone reading this chapter will already be well into their fifties, and looking ahead only a few years to their retirement. No one ever really thinks of planning ahead to the day they stop work, until they are quite close to that date. Earlier in life there is too much to do – getting married, finding a house, bringing up a family, enjoying foreign travel, buying a proper car, climbing up the career ladder. Then, just when you think you have got it all, retirement looms up on the horizon and you start to see your income fall again.

Our perception of retirement has changed over the course of the last 50 years. Two generations ago, when our grandparents retired, the last section of their life was seen as the most difficult. Giving up work meant giving up your income at the end of a long hard life when they had been lucky to keep body and soul together let alone try to save anything for later years. So retirement meant a severe fall in living standards.

Not so nowadays. Many couples look forward to the day they pocket the gold watch and switch off the alarm clock. They look ahead to using the free time for charity work, or to do all the things they have never had time for – indulging hobbies, travelling, taking up new pursuits and widening their horizons. But to do that they need money. Few people of this generation would welcome a severe drop in living standards when they retire.

Nor should they. Company pensions, if you have had one long enough, should give you sufficient for a decent retirement life style. You might have to sell the Jaguar and buy a Metro, but you shouldn't have to start taking the bus.

So what should you do in the years before retirement to make sure you are set up financially for the golden years?

There are three main money areas to check out:
- pensions
- investments
- debts

PENSIONS

For most people, the pension will be the main source of income once they retire. The state retirement pension, maybe a SERPS or graduated state pension top up and, perhaps, a company or private pension. But will that be enough for your day to day living expenses? Work it out.

State pension

All OAPs qualify for the basic state pension, providing they have paid enough National Insurance contributions while they worked. That means men must have worked and contributed for 44 years between the ages of 16 and 65, while women must have contributed for 39 years. However, even if you weren't working you will get credit for things like retiring early, being in full time education, being unemployed or claiming child benefit.

What you get, at the moment, is £52 per person if you are claiming on your own contributions, £31.25 if you are claiming on your spouse's. So a married couple, claiming on the husband's contributions, will get £83.25 a week. That figure goes up every year.

Gaps in your record If you have been working abroad, or gave up work voluntarily and have gaps in your NI record, you can pay extra now to qualify for a bigger pension when you retire. You will have to pay what are known as Class 3 NI payments, currently £5.05 a week. You can go back six years to fill gaps in your record, but no more. Write to the DSS and ask what you owe.

SERPS and Graduated State Pension

These are the additions to your pension which will increase your state pension if you are in the schemes. Graduated State pensions came first (from 1961 to 1975), and in 1978 SERPS (State Earnings Related Pension Scheme) were launched. The more you earn, up to certain limits, the more pension entitlement you will get.

In 1988 the Government changed the way of calculating SERPS. If you retire this century it won't affect you, if you retire next century it will. By how much depends on the year in which you retire. Unless you have an Einstein-type brain you won't be able to work out your entitlement, but don't worry, the man at the DSS will do it for you. Fill in form NP 38 and you should get some idea of how much you will get when you retire.

Company and Private Pensions

If you have been wise you will have a tidy sum coming to you from your own pension. This will either be a company pension – perhaps several company pensions if you moved jobs a lot – or a private pension plan.

There are two types of company pensions: final salary and money purchase.

Final salary This is the most common and guarantees you a pension based on the salary you earn in your last year before retirement. Usually it is 1/60th or 1/40th of your final year's salary, multiplied by the number of years you have worked with the firm, up to a maximum of two-thirds of your pay. If you joined the scheme after 14 March 1989 there is also a limit to how much of your salary you can use – around £100 000.

Money purchase schemes These don't relate to your salary. They are funds built up from contributions from the employer and, usually, the employee. When the employee retires his fund is used to buy a pension scheme from an insurance company.

If you have a private pension plan it will run along money purchase lines in that your contributions will build up a fund that will eventually buy you a pension, but it is unlikely that your employer will contribute anything to it.

With all the above schemes, write to the company or department running the pension scheme, and ask for an estimate of how much you will get out when you retire.

By now you should have some idea of how much you will have coming in when you retire. On top of that there might be two other factors to consider:

Age allowance If you are 65 when you retire you might qualify for age allowance, so your tax bill will go down (see page 64 for full details).

Part time job If you are going to continue to work on a part time basis you will have more coming in than just your pensions so add that into your calculations.

Spending

Once you retire, your spending habits will change. Some things you will spend more on, others much less. For example, your outgoings on clothes will go down because you don't need suits and smart outfits for work; daily travel will fall as you don't commute to and from the office or factory; you will spend less on lunches, drinks after work, contributions to leaving and marriage presents and sponsorship forms.

Other things will go up. You will have to heat the house more during the day; your telephone bill might rise now that you don't have the use of the office facility; you will spend more on day to day living, hobbies and treats that you now have time for. But the one big thing in your favour is that you can take advantage of cheap deals: everything from flying off peak to getting your hair cut on a Monday or Tuesday when it's cheaper. You will, in fact, start using your time to save money instead of using money to save time.

AVCs

Now that you have worked out your likely pension income, and given some thought to what your day to day expenses could come to, you should have some idea of whether or not you will have enough to manage on when retirement day comes. You might, of course, also have some savings, but in general I wouldn't add that into your equation. Few pensioners like to use their capital to live on. They see it as rainy day money for when they are much older and might need the fund.

If your pension is not going to be large enough, you must do something now, while you are still working. You must increase your pension entitlement. The main vehicle for doing this is through an AVC – an Additional Voluntary Contribution. Every year you can pay up to 15 per cent of your gross salary into a pension policy (more if you are self employed). Very few of us do that. So there should be plenty of scope for you to pay in extra in any one year. AVCs can be regular, spasmodic or one-off payments, whatever you like, provided you keep the total below 15 per cent of your salary. If you don't want to pay them into the company scheme take out an FSAVC – a Free Standing Additional Voluntary Contribution and it just means the money is going into a different scheme.

You can make AVCs or FSAVCs at any time in your working life, but for most people it is something to be done towards the end of their working life when the children are off their hands, the mortgage is a smaller percentage of their income and they have a bit more money around.

Pensions are very tax efficient because, unless you are an extremely high earner, all the money going in, growing within and coming out of the pension scheme is tax free. You don't get that in any other savings medium. The downside of the pension is that it won't be paid to you until you retire. So don't over-fund it because you can't get the money out again. Retiring early just to unlock your pension would be a bit drastic.

INVESTMENT

Investment-wise, you are standing at a crossroads. You have come through decades of struggling to make ends meet and not wanting to risk anything, and emerged into a time when you are prepared to gamble a little of your money. Once you retire, you go back into that mode of no-risk money management. What you have when you retire has to do you for the rest of your days so you don't want to risk any of it on a hare-brained scheme that might not be that profitable anyway.

In your fifties, however, you might feel that a bit of risk is worthwhile. How much risk you are prepared to take, depends on how much you are prepared to lose. I always think that if you are investing in shares, or anything riskier, you should assume you will lose the lot. If you don't that is a bonus. But if you start with that attitude it will stop you investing what you cannot afford to lose. Full details on some of the options open to you are in Chapter 9.

The closer you come to retirement, the less risk you will want to take. If you invest in shares, or unit trusts, you will find over the years that you have had a few winners, and a few losers. By the time you hit 60 or 65 you will not want to punt on the losers, only the winners. Life is not like that. Avoiding the losers means getting out of the game, so move your money to the safe haven of high interest bank and building society accounts, or try gilts. Pick suitable stock that you can hold to redemption and get a good capital gain, but if they go up sharply in the meantime you can sell at a profit. Details of gilts and how to buy them are on page 80.

This is the time, too, to rationalise your investments. Over the years you may have built up a plethora of bank and building society accounts, you might have a couple of current accounts, four or five savings books, maybe three or four credit cards and a handful of store cards. But do you need them all? Probably not. Cut out the ones you don't need or want. And that in itself will save you a bit now that credit cards are nearly all costing you upwards of £10 a year.

Keep your affairs simple – it is easier for you to look after now and for someone else to cope with should something happen to you.

DEBTS
It is nice to go into retirement with a clean slate – owing nothing to anybody. But it doesn't always work out that way so don't get rid of a debt just for the psychological boost it will give you.

Mortgage
The guidelines on mortgages are quite simple to follow.

Repayments If you have a repayment mortgage in the last four years of its life, and you have enough capital to pay it off with ease, then do so. You are not getting much tax relief by now because it is mainly capital not interest that you are repaying so you are probably paying more in interest than you are getting on your savings. However, don't borrow to pay off the mortgage, as a mortgage is still the cheapest form of borrowing there is. And don't use all your capital to pay it off either. You can't get the mortgage back again if you find in future you need a loan to buy a new car, or fund a trip to Australia or whatever.

Endowment Don't pay off an endowment mortgage, let it run its course. The endowment insurance policy running alongside the mortgage comes into its own in the last few years and earns big money so keep paying the premiums and you could find yourself with a tidy lump sum after you have paid off the mortgage. If you are not going to be able to afford the mortgage after you retire, go and see your lender to find out what your options are, and turn to page 100, for further advice.

Other loans Paying off other bank and HP loans early will probably cost you up to two months' payments extra. So work out for yourself if it is worthwhile.

New debts Once you retire you will find that you may need to take out a loan for, say, a car if you had to give back the company one. Prepare early for this. Start putting away cash now to build up a lump sum that can either be used to make the purchase or to help fund the payments.

If there are any major household appliances likely to need replacing in the near future, try to do it while you are still working. It is easier to make monthly payments for these while you are still working, than when you retire. Don't think that you can use the lump sum that comes with your pension to buy the new car, put in a fitted kitchen and pay for the holiday of a lifetime. Of course it might be able to do all that, but in reality it is your bankroll for retirement and you can only spend it once. If you use it up within the first few months of retirement, you won't have it for the next 10 to 20 years when you are more likely to need it.

FINANCIAL ADVICE

You might feel at this stage you want to take professional financial advice. And that can be a good idea. Even if you have read this whole book, and absorbed most of it, there will still be a lot of help you can get from the right person. He or she will be used to dealing with people in similar circumstances to you and will, or should, know the best deals around.

But don't take everything they say unquestioningly. They could be wrong, they could be a rogue out to get your cash, they may be making an inappropriate judgement. So think about what they have said before you blithely sign away your money.

Before you go to a professional money adviser, work out what you want from him or her. What sort of investment are you looking for, how much risk will you take, what sort of return will you hope to get, when will you need to get the money back? These are the sort of questions you should have already asked yourself.

The professional adviser should ask you some fairly detailed questions about your money affairs in order to be able to give you the 'best advice' – and that is what they are legally bound to do.

If the adviser is 'tied' they can only sell products in one particular company. If the adviser is 'independent' they can sell from any company. Make sure you know in advance which you are with.

Cost No one works for nothing – not you, not me and not the professional adviser. If you are not given a bill at the end, it is because the adviser gets his money from commission. The company whose product you are sold, pays the commission to the adviser. Some products such as endowment policies pay a lot more than others such as unit trusts. Ask the adviser what the commission rate is, so that you know you are not being sold one particular plan just for the better rate that the adviser will get.

If you are getting your advice from a professional such as an accountant or solicitor, and are paying an hourly fee for that service, then the commission should be paid to you, or offset against the final bill. Make sure it is.

If the adviser is independent, make sure he or she is a full member of SIB (071 283 2474). It should be on the letter heading, but you can check by phoning the organisation and asking or you can look up the SIB register on Teletext or at your nearest main library.

TIP · Don't be rushed into buying something. If the deal is so good it won't wait 12 hours while you think about it, move on to another deal.

Whatever advice you are offered, think about it. Use this book to check out what has been put forward, ask plenty of questions and if you think the idea is good, go ahead. But remember, there really is only one person who has your financial interest at heart. That is you. So if the plan doesn't satisfy you, move on.

Countdown to Retirement
Twenties
Think about a pension – the earlier you start the less you have to put in to get a good payout at the end. If your employer's scheme lets you in, take up the offer.
Thirties
Join a pension scheme now if you are not already in one. Go for your employer's if you can, otherwise start a Personal Pension Plan.
Forties
Job changers should make sure that they get a good deal on their pension. It should be a higher priority than an extra few pounds on their salary.
Fifties
Look at your investments and go for capital growth with your money. Your salary should provide all the income you need. Check that you and your

spouse are up to date with NI contributions, and pay Class 3 if you are not. Think about AVCs if you need to boost your pension. If you feel your house will be too big for you to look after in your old age, move now. It is good to establish yourself in the new area a few years before you retire.
Sixties (or late fifties for women)
Check that your pension is going to be large enough for you to live on. If it is not then do something about it now. Think about any big purchases you have to make, and try to put the money aside while you are still working. Start to move your investments into less risky accounts.

18 · *The Golden Years*

For most of our working life we look forward to our retirement day, the onset of a time when we can do what we enjoy, and enjoy what we are doing. It won't be so much fun if there is no money in the bank so it is worthwhile, quite early on in your golden years, getting the cash sorted out.

Being in control of your cash is still important. More so now, because you have to budget your money to last you to the end of your days. The problem, of course, is that you don't know how long that will be. You could pop your clogs tomorrow, or live on in fine fettle to receive your 100th birthday telegram from the Queen (or King!). You neither want to live a poverty-stricken retirement and die rich, nor do you want to have several 'big spender' years and then live on in distress for the rest of your days. It is a juggling act – and the trick is not to drop the balls.

FIRST THINGS FIRST

Initially, you have to know where you stand financially. You will need to know if your monthly income is enough to keep you; whether the surplus will cover high days, holidays and hobbies; how much capital you have, and whether or not you need the income from the capital (or, indeed, the capital itself), to supplement your monthly income.

1 If you retired at the regular retirement age of 65 for men and 60 for women you will probably have the state retirement pension and a company or personal pension. Is that enough to cover your everyday needs?

Yes . . . Move on to Number 3

No . . . You will need to supplement your income and there are several ways to do that. You could take a part time job; take in a lodger; use your house to provide income for you through a home income or reversion plan (details below), or invest your capital for income.

2 Investing for income means putting any savings that you have in an account which pays the highest rate of interest you can get, and withdrawing the interest to supplement your weekly or monthly income. You could do it yourself, or you could use a building society, bank or National Savings monthly income account to do it for you. You will get slightly less interest if it's paid monthly (either sent to you by cheque or paid into another account), but it is a handy way of working.

Try not to use the capital unless you have to because once it is spent there will be no more income from it.

> *TIP ·* If you are a non-tax payer, remember to sign an exemption form at your bank or building society branch otherwise you will be losing 25 per cent of the interest unnecessarily.

3 Investing your nest egg for later years means trying to get capital growth on the money, though you will want to keep the risk to a minimum. No one wants to lose any of the cash that has to see them through the golden years, so don't put it into anything risky. If someone offers you a deal where you will get a better return than looks possible, ask yourself why a good fairy should choose you. If the deal is that good they would keep it for themselves. Most of the people that lose cash in dodgy deals do so because they were greedy for a better return than was really possible.

Go for high interest savings accounts, or gilts, or perhaps unit or investment trusts if you feel prepared to take a small gamble. Remember that if you commute part of your pension to a lump sum – as most people do – that lump sum is to keep you in future years not to pay for a Caribbean cruise.

4 If you haven't enough to live on, and have very little in the way of savings, you might be able to get help from the DSS. Go down to the local office yourself, or ask at the CAB for help. They will be able to work out if you are entitled to anything, and going to the CAB can be a lot less daunting than trying to deal with the DSS.

GETTING OLDER

As you get older your spending pattern changes again. You will need less money for things like holidays and outings, because you won't feel like going on so many. Eventually you may become too old to drive and you will sell the car.

But you will probably spend more on medicines, although prescriptions are free, and visits to hospitals. You will take taxis where previously you took the bus, and you will have to start paying for things that you used to do yourself, such as gardening, window cleaning, cleaning the house, perhaps even laundry and shopping. For that reason most old people try to keep a tidy capital sum for their very old age.

Others find themselves becoming what is known as 'house rich, cash poor'. It means that they own a substantial property, worth quite a lot, but they can't afford to keep it in good repair and they don't want to move. There is a solution, but think carefully about this step before you take it.

Home Income and Reversion Policies

If your most valuable asset is your home, and you would like to cash in on it, but continue to live out your days there, consider this:

Home Income Plan – This type of plan allows you to raise a loan on your home. You use this cash sum to buy an annuity which will give you a regular monthly income for the rest of your life (no matter how long you live) and pay the interest on the loan. On your death (or the death of the surviving spouse if you are married), the loan is repaid from the sale of the home.

The older you are the more you will get – because statistically you will live for a shorter time – but for the figures to make sense you have to be over 69, if you are single, and over 70 (with a combined age of 145), if you are married.

Typically, a couple aged 78 and 72, with a house worth £45 000, raising a maximum of £30 000 on their home could expect an annual income of £1006 if they are tax payers, or £1246 if they are non-tax payers, which they are more likely to be.

These schemes are ideal for those who want to pass something on to their heirs, because once the loan is repaid, on death, the rest of the value of the house goes into the estate to be distributed according to the will.

Home Reversion Scheme – This is a slightly different animal and can be more suited to those who don't want to leave anything after their death. With Home Reversion schemes you sell all or part of your home in return for an income for life and a life tenancy. On your death the house, or the percentage of it you have sold, goes to the reversion company. The big advantage is that you are not taking out a loan so there is no interest to pay. As such, you will get a larger monthly income. The drawback is that you are signing over all, or part, of your house.

The 78- and 72-year-old couple using a reversion scheme instead of a home income plan would get £1335 a year from selling 75 per cent of their £45 000 home, £1500 if they are non-tax payers. Ideally, you should use a plan that is linked to the value of properties so that your income rises with property values. There are a few schemes which give a cash sum, rather than an annuity.

Schemes to avoid – As with investments, at this time of your life you don't want to take any risk with your home. So don't use schemes that include Roll Up Loans or Investment Bonds. On paper they may seem a good deal as you appear to get a larger income, but if interest rates or investment decisions turn against you, you may end up having to sell up to pay bills.

To qualify for home income plans or reversion schemes, you have to own a home that has no outstanding mortgage on it and if you are on Income Support, or Community Charge Benefit, you might lose some of your benefit when your monthly income rises.

Never go for one of those schemes without discussing it with your lawyer, and it may also be a good idea to chat it over with your family.

Further details are available in a helpful book called *Using Your Home As Capital* published by Age Concern (address on page 149).

MOVING ON

There might come a time – early or late in retirement – when you want to move out of your family home. It might just be that it is too big for you to run or it might be problems of health that force you to move.

For many, sheltered accommodation is the next step: either council run (though they can be a bit thin on the ground), or in the private sector. You still have a place of your own, but there is generally a warden on site, or an alarm system you can ring, if you are in any difficulty. If you are buying in the private sector, and need a mortgage, you could go for an interest-only loan. That means that you just pay the interest during the life of the loan, and at the end (probably on your death) the flat would be sold and the capital repaid.

Interest-only loans are usually a little more expensive than ordinary mortgages. Detailed advice about buying sheltered housing is contained in an Age Concern booklet called *A Buyer's Guide to Sheltered Housing.*

Residential and nursing homes may be the next step. If you go into a home in the private sector you will be told the price at the outset, and you can work out for yourself if you can afford it.

In the public sector are local authority residential homes. Don't image that just because they are run by the local authority they will be free of charge. They are not. What you pay depends on how much capital and income you have. Each local authority has a standard weekly charge. How much of that you pay depends on this formula: for every £50 of capital you have, you pay 25p a week towards the charge. So if you have savings of £9500 you would pay 9500 ÷ 50 = 190 × 25p = £47.50. And that is what you would pay per week towards the cost of the weekly charge. On top of that you would have to hand over your income, probably your state pension. When your capital reduces to £1500 it will stop being considered.

The weekly charge is usually equal to the single person's state pension and if that is all the money you have – and you are giving it to the home then the DSS will pay you Income Support as a sort of pocket money.

Age Concern have a series of helpful factsheets, which are free and worth having and which detail residential and nursing home care and who qualifies for Income Support. Available from 1268 London Road, London SW16 4EJ, for England and Wales, and 54a Fountainbridge, Edinburgh EH3 9PT (031 228 5656), for Scotland.

YOU CAN'T TAKE IT WITH YOU

There are no pockets in shrouds, or so they say. Whatever fortune, large or small, you have amassed during your life you can't take it with you when you go. But you can have a good say as to where the money goes, whether it is Fulham Football Club or the family. Make sure, if you haven't already done so, that you write a will. And if you wrote your will a long time ago, check it over to see that what you said then is still valid now.

If the value of your home has gone up dramatically over the years, you might find yourself within the realms of Inheritance Tax. At present, an estate becomes liable for Inheritance Tax when it is worth more than £140 000 – though that figure goes up every year, roughly in line with inflation. Anyone with a house worth as much as this should do some tax planning to avoid giving unnecessary cash to the Inland Revenue (for more details see page 90).

Of course there is no point in taking a week to get everything sorted out if no one knows where any of your documents are. Once you die, you can't come back to leave messages like, 'The key is in the bureau drawer', so leave a note while you are alive. In fact, why not leave a Life Plan?

━━━━━━━━━━━━━━━━ *Life Plan* ━━━━━━━━━━━━━━━━

My Will is to be found . . . .

. . . .

. . . .

Other important documents are kept . . . .

. . . .

. . . .

Pension details . . . .

. . . .

. . . .

Life assurance policy details . . . .
. . . .
. . . .

House and mortgage details . . . .
. . . .
. . . .

Insurance details . . . .
. . . .
. . . .

Savings accounts . . . .
. . . .
. . . .

Shares, unit trusts etc . . . .
. . . .
. . . .

Tax office . . . .
. . . .
. . . .

In the event of my death please contact . . . .
. . . .
. . . .

Useful Addresses

Chapter 5 · How to Borrow Money
Association of British Credit Unions, 48 Maddox Street, London W1R 9BB

National Federation of Savings and Cooperative Credit Unions, 1st Floor, Jacob's Well, Bradford BD1 5RW

Chapter 6 · When Credit Becomes Debt
Directory of Social Change, Radius Works, Back Lane, London NW3 1HL

National Debtline, Birmingham Settlement, 318 Summer Lane, Birmingham B19 3RL   Tel: 021 359 8501

Chapter 9 · Building Bricks
Unit Trust Association, 65 Kingsway, London WC2B 6TD
Tel: 071 831 0898

Association of Investment Trust Companies, Park House, 16 Finsbury Circus, London EC2M 7JJ   Tel: 071 588 5347

Chapter 11 · Buying Your First Home
The Housing Corporation, 149 Tottenham Court Road, London WC1P 0BN   Tel: 071 387 9466

Chapter 13 · Children and Money
Department of Education and Science, Room 3/65 Elizabeth House, York Road, London SE1 7PH; Welsh Office Educational Department, Crown Offices, Cathays Park, Cardiff CF1 3NQ; Scottish Education Department, Room 4/25 New St Andrew's House, St James Centre, Edinburgh EH1 3SY

Instant Muscle, 84 North End Road, London W14 93F
Tel: 071 603 2504

Livewire, 60 Grainger Street, Newcastle Upon Tyne
Tel: 091 261 5584

Chapter 14 · Separation and Divorce
The Divorce Registry, Somerset House, Strand, London WC2

Family Mediators' Association, The Old House, Rectory Gardens,
Henbury, Bristol BS10 7AQ   Tel: 0272 500140

Chapter 18 · The Golden Years
Age Concern, 1268 London Road, London SW16 4EJ (for England
and Wales) and 54a Fountainbridge, Edinburgh EH3 9PT (for
Scotland)   Tel: 031 228 5656

Useful Leaflets

Chapter 6 · When Credit Becomes Debt
A Guide to Grants for Individuals in Need obtainable from: Directory of
Social Change, Radius Works, Back Lane, London NW3 1HL
Insolvency Act 1986 – A Guide to Bankruptcy Law obtainable from:
Insolvency Service 2–14 Bunhill Row, London ECY 8LL

Chapter 10 · Understanding Your Tax
Inland Revenue booklet:
IH 1 Inheritance Tax

Chapter 12 · Becoming a Mum
DSS leaflets:
N1 17A *A Guide to Maternity Benefits*
FB 8 *Babies and Benefits* (which has an application form for Maternity
Allowance, Child Benefit and One Parent Benefit)
FB 27 *Bringing up Children?*
CH 11 *One Parent Benefit*
AC 2 *Now there is an easier way to get your Child Benefit*

Chapter 14 · Separation and Divorce
Inland Revenue leaflet:
IR 93 *Income Tax, Separation, Divorce and Maintenance Payments*

Chapter 15 · Becoming a Widow
DSS leaflets:
D 49 *What to do after a death*
NI 51 *National Insurance for Widows*
NP 45 *A Guide to Widows' Benefits*
FB 29 *Help when Someone Dies*
Inland Revenue leaflet:
IR 91 *Independent Taxation – A Guide for Widows and Widowers*

Chapter 16 · Redundancy and Unemployment
Employee's Rights on Insolvency of Employer

Chapter 18 · The Golden Years
Age Concern leaflet:
Using your Home as Capital
Age Concern booklet:
A Buyer's Guide to Sheltered Housing
Age Concern factsheets on residential and nursing home care and who
qualifies for Income Support, all obtainable from Age Concern,
1268 London Road, London SW16 4EJ (for England and Wales) and
54a Fountainbridge, Edinburgh EH3 9PT   Tel: 031 228 5656 (for
Scotland)

All Inland Revenue leaflets mentioned above are available, free of
charge, from your local Inland Revenue office. All DSS leaflets are
available, free of charge, from your local DSS office.

Index